What About Other Faiths?

What About Other Faiths?

Is Jesus Christ the Only Way to God?

Martin Goldsmith

Hodder & Stoughton
LONDON SYDNEY AUCKLAND

Copyright © 1989, 2002 by Martin Goldsmith

First published in 1989
This edition first published in 2003

The right of Martin Goldsmith to be identified as
the Author of the Work has been asserted by him in accordance
with the Copyright, Designs and Patents Act 1988.

10 9 8 7 6 5 4 3 2 1

British Library Cataloguing in Publication Data
A record for this book is available from the British Library

ISBN 0 340 86150 9

Typeset by Avon Dataset Ltd, Bidford-on-Avon, Warks

Printed and bound in Great Britain by
Clays Ltd, St Ives plc

Hodder & Stoughton
A Division of Hodder Headline Ltd
338 Euston Road
London NW1 3BH
www.madaboutbooks.com

Contents

1

What About Other Faiths?

The mission drew to a close. The last week had seen large central meetings, informal coffee parties in people's homes, and impromptu discussions with earnest debates in the evenings. Now it was all over and the team of workers returned to their homes. But in their minds they continued to ponder all that had happened. Some of them met to share their impressions to see whether new lessons could be learned.

'It was strange how the questions people asked differed totally from what used to be discussed,' one worker commented. 'None of the usual arguments even came up in the meetings I attended.'

One of the less experienced young people asked with curiosity, 'What used to be the debates in earlier years? What issues did you expect to be raised?'

The old hands answered with the superior attitude of those who state the obvious, 'Well, you know, the old chestnuts of whether the Bible is full of mistakes; and don't science and the Bible contradict each other?' They all agreed that such battles had dominated religious debate in the past. But times have changed and today's questions relate to the cultural streams of our society.

The little group of Christian workers was amazed to find that not one of them had encountered a single question in any discussion related to these formerly heated topics of the reliability of scripture and the relationship of the Bible to science and evolution.

'How sad,' one of them commented reflectively, 'so much of our Christian literature and preaching still struggles with those issues.' They laughed together at the tragic tendency of Christians to answer questions no one is asking or at least to answer them long after they have become irrelevant.

They then began to ask each other what hot potatoes had scorched their fingers during the mission. It seemed that two basic questions had predominated.

1. Two Questions

a) What is?

As the evening continued, coffee and biscuits loosened tongues and the guests began to talk freely. One rather artistic-looking man voiced his doubts, 'I find it hard to believe that anything in this world actually exists.' Another person backed him up by pointing out that you could not prove existence. Descartes' *cogito, ergo sum*, 'I think, therefore I am', did not quite seem to meet the situation: or perhaps it did, for soon the younger people present began to apply their philosophical queries to themselves. Some questioned their own existence. How can we actually be sure that life is not one big dream? Was Descartes right that the act of thinking demonstrates that we really are? Or do we have to take seriously the Asian story about the man who dreamed he was a butterfly? The story implies that it could equally well have been a butterfly dreaming it was a man – and that man would also be dreaming! Or is life just one big unreal dream in which both man and butterfly share in non-existence? Is there anything or anybody which actually is?

More traditional Westerners may smile at such debates, for they stem from Eastern philosophies and worldviews which differ radically from our backgrounds. But many more thinking people of the younger generation have been deeply influenced by Eastern religious thought. It is therefore of vital importance that Christian theology, biblical teaching and preaching should not only answer the questions of previous generations, but also address the battles of today and of the future. We must scratch where people itch.

In the West heated debates have raged about the historicity of the Creation story in Genesis. Is it just a mythical account or can it somehow be squared with scientific and geological research? Such questions may touch raw nerves with some of us, but in the context of Eastern religious philosophical influence the Creation story has a totally different significance.

In the Bible the first chapters of Genesis speak of a God who is personal and active in creation of the world. We see a God who truly is and who imparts something of his nature to his Creation. We may deduce therefore that the universe also is. And particularly we read that God made humankind in his own likeness, his own image. If God truly is, then humankind shares the characteristic of existence with him. So we can freely claim that we are. In the light of the Genesis Creation account we need no longer doubt whether anything is, nor whether we ourselves exist.

In Exodus 3:13 Moses openly confesses his anxiety to his God. The Lord was commanding him to go to the people of Israel, deliver them from the slavery and oppression of Pharaoh and lead them out from Egypt towards the promised land of Canaan. But would the people of Israel accept him? How would they know that God had truly sent him? Moses asks God what he should reply if the Jews asked him what God's name is, what God's nature is like. God then reveals himself to Moses, saying, ' "I AM WHO I AM" ' and orders Moses to declare to the people of Israel that ' "I AM has sent me to you" ' (v. 14).

Commentators have struggled to define the significance of this name of God. The Jewish philosopher and theologian Martin Buber suggests that it signifies a God who is present with his people. In the danger of confrontation with Pharaoh and the might of Egypt, Moses and his people needed to know that God is not an inactive and distant deity. Buber believes therefore that the name signifies 'I am there'. Moses' God will accompany him as he goes to the court of Pharaoh to demand 'Let my people go'; God will go with Israel in the exodus from Egypt and in their trials as they move towards Canaan. Buber's explanation of the meaning of the name 'I am' tallies with what we know of God's nature and what he does for his people. He is indeed the God who never leaves and never forsakes his children.

But perhaps we might suggest a further possible significance in this great title 'I am'. While the Egyptians worship mythical deities who have no genuine reality or existence, the God of Israel is alive and true. He truly exists. If God truly is, he can also do things. Therefore Moses and the people of Israel can be comforted by the reassuring knowledge of a God who is active on behalf of his followers, who genuinely is.

It is significant that Jesus claimed the same title of 'I am' for himself. We see this particularly in John's Gospel with the so-called 'I am' sayings – 'I am the good shepherd', 'I am the vine', 'I am the resurrection and the life', 'Before Abraham was, I am', etc. In Jesus the Messiah the God who is takes flesh and lives visibly on earth. It is finally in relationship to Jesus that we experience how we too have a sure and true existence in the Creator God – 'For in him we live and move and have our being' (Acts 17:28).

One wonders whether those young people will find the answer to their questions through the God who is the great 'I am'. Will they discover the way to know 'I am' through Jesus who has made God known (John 1:18)? They truly are because of the God who is. He made them in his own image. And in

Jesus he has shown himself to them so that they can come to know him for themselves.

b) Why Christianity?

While the young people's first question reflects the pervasive influence of Eastern religions, their second topic for debate goes wider. Again and again the issue of 'other religions' comes up. Can we believe in Jesus Christ and the Christian faith when there are so many other religious possibilities? How can we be sure that the Christian answers provide the truth when other religions offer different approaches? While these uncertainties are openly voiced by many young adults, they also reflect the underlying feelings of many older Church members too – and of many people who reject the Christian message.

As we shall see in a later chapter, many theologians today query the traditional Christian view that Jesus Christ is in any meaningful way unique. They suggest that God's truth is reflected in all religions to some extent and it is therefore presumptuous and wrong to make any claims to absolute truth. We all need to become better people within the boundaries of our own religious traditions, they assert, but no one should seek to convert the followers of other faiths. This view has percolated through to many RE teachers and Church ministers. Through them it influences the average Christian and many outside the Church too.

Let me give an example. A good friend of mine went to a professional conference in the Middle East some years ago. She is highly intelligent, a top person in her line of work, but still a relatively young Christian. Until she visited the Middle East she had assumed that all faiths are basically as good as each other, so she expected to enjoy her first-hand experience of a Muslim society. It came as a great shock to find that actually she reacted strongly against much of what she saw. This negative experience of another culture and religion has put a question mark against her whole philosophy of life and is making her look again at what her Christian faith really teaches about other religions. In the next chapter we shall try to examine what the Bible says on this subject.

The teaching of comparative religion in our schools has much to commend it, but it tends to underline the idea that all religions have much in common and are of equal validity as ways to know God. Such teaching usually avoids mention of radical disagreements between the different faiths. It generally prefers to stress common beliefs and experience rather than debating opposite positions held by the different religions.

Even in areas of our country which lack a multi-cultural and multi-religious mix of population, nobody today can avoid becoming aware of other religious traditions. The teaching of religion compels all children to learn about the different faiths – and this is essential in our country today, for it is of primary importance that all our different communities learn to understand each other better. But it does also mean that all our children grow up with an awareness that Christianity is by no means the only alternative.

The media also strongly oppose any exclusive claims to truth. A clear assurance of belief is frequently attacked with the pejorative terms 'fundamentalism' or 'intolerance', whereas agnostic doubt is assumed to be reasonable and peace-loving. Actually, as we shall see, liberal 'tolerance' often demonstrates an aggressive intolerance towards all whose sure faith disagrees with their lack of spiritual commitment. Since 11 September 2001 and the consequent fear of religious extremism evangelical Christian faith has been lumped together with Muslim fundamentalism. It is therefore politically incorrect to believe in Jesus Christ as God's unique way of salvation or the Bible as God's supreme revealed word to all humanity. In coming days there is a real danger hovering like a Damocles sword over evangelicals' heads. Evangelical Christians could face discrimination and even persecution at the hands of so-called liberals. It could easily become illegal in Europe for a Christian church or institution to insist on only employing Christians and indeed Christians who live up to certain moral standards in their private lives.

We have already noted the importance of scratching where people itch. In our preaching, teaching and witness therefore we need to tackle the burning question of the relationship of the Christian faith to other religions. What does the Bible have to say about this? What do some of our current Church leaders think on this topic? And how do we relate biblical views to the world of our day? Terrorism in the name of Islam and inter-religious fighting in the Middle East have forced people to ask serious religious questions. Islam particularly has become the centre of debate and questioning. Inevitably we have to ask ourselves how Christians relate to Islam and Muslims. Jewish questions about prophecy and the state of Israel now come high on the agenda and we need too to ask what shari'ah (Islamic Law) has to say about the land of Israel/Palestine. Christians cannot afford to avoid such questions today. The Church must not become an ostrich with its head in the sand.

2. Why the Questions?

That Church mission highlighted two basic points of discussion on religion. Both arise from the modern situation of a mixed society. No longer can the adherent of one faith ignore all the others.

Eastern religious influence

In the discussion concerning existence we detect the underlying influence of Hinduism in particular.

In classical Hindu philosophy the story is told of a man who thought he saw a coiled-up snake in the half-light of the evening. But when more light was brought, he became aware that in reality it was just a coil of rope. This story reveals the various levels of reality, of what is.

It could be said that the coiled snake is. In the mind of the man that snake was a reality and it influenced his thoughts and his course of action. With the karmic law of cause and effect everything he thought or did has continuing repercussions, so it is highly significant. To some extent then we may say that the snake is a reality, but it is a rather superficial existence which is merely apparent. The existence of the snake is an illusion.

At a somewhat less illusory level of existence we might affirm that the coil of rope is. In the full daylight we can touch and observe it, assuring ourselves that it really is a rope. We might say that the rope is historically true and real.

But the Hindu would say that even the existence of the coil of rope is an illusion. In the limited realm of the historical we can only see at a superficial level of reality. Actually, he would declare, only the ultimate Absolute of Brahman is. All else is an illusion. There is no duality of Brahman and other beings or things. Only Brahman exists. Brahman is the ultimate *Tat Sat*, 'It Is'. Neither the writer nor the reader of this book actually is; in fact this book itself does not exist except at the superficial historical level of the coil of rope. Enlightenment comes when you become aware that all is Brahman, that neither you nor anything else has any separate existence.

Classical Buddhism feels that Hinduism has compromised with a cowardly failure to face ultimate truth. In the highest form of Buddhism even Brahman does not exist. Nothing is. The ultimate reality is *Sunyata*, 'the Void'. This concept is seen in the doctrine of *Anatta*, 'No Self'.

The Buddha taught this doctrine by asking his disciple to bring him a chariot. The disciple was commanded to remove one part after another of the chariot until nothing remained. Then the Buddha asked his disciple, 'Where is the chariot?'

The answer came, 'There is no chariot, master.'

So the Buddha taught the doctrine that ultimately nothing is. There is no chariot; there is no disciple; there is nothing and nobody.

We cannot doubt that Hindu and Buddhist thought have permeated deeply into the Western worldview. This has been confirmed by a report that some twenty-five per cent of British people now believe in the Eastern religious doctrine of reincarnation. We see this further reflected in the popularity of the 'New Age' movement and in the spate of television dramas and films which show the hero or heroine in the contemporary life and also in a previous reincarnation. Where does this Eastern religious influence stem from?

i) Effect on ordinary people

In the heady days of cultural questioning in the 1960s the Beatles and others blazed the guru trail. Their example, projected by the mass media, influenced many ordinary people, who followed in their footsteps to seek a new spirituality to fit the new cultural mood. Interest in the life of Hinduism and Buddhism led to the import into the West of various forms of Eastern meditation and yoga. These and other spiritualistic activities leading to trance-like peace gave to their followers a new feeling of relief from the tensions of normal daily life. This fitted well with the drug culture, for that too helped to bring people out from their separate self-existence and give them an experience of new spiritual dimensions. As the years have passed, the range of yogic and meditational practices has widened, and 'New Age' ideas have been introduced, particularly the use of martial arts and alternative medicine linked to Eastern religious practices and verbal formulas.

Some of these Eastern religious practices have also been brought into the life of the Christian Church. In some cases this has been positive, for in many churches quiet meditation was unknown or little used. But there has also been the danger of syncretism, mixing the Christian faith with alien elements without sufficiently converting the theological base of those new practices. We have to ask what people actually understand by the word 'meditation'. Do they mean such concentration on the object of meditation that their minds go beyond it into peaceful emptiness? Or are they meditating on something which has value in itself? Do they then retain full mental awareness, praising God through Jesus Christ with their minds as well as their spirit? Meditation can be either Christian or Buddhist.

So the use of Eastern religious practices has led to the wide spread of Hindu and Buddhist concepts within our society.

ii) The academic world

In more academic circles Eastern religions have increasingly permeated the very foundations of Western philosophy. Already in the early days of rationalism writers like Rousseau and Voltaire refer to the debates of the early Jesuit missionary Ricci in China who struggled with the relationship of Christianity to Confucianism. Ricci concluded that truth was also to be found in Confucian wisdom as well as in Christianity, so there is a source of divine knowledge beyond the boundaries of the Christian Church and the Bible.

In more recent history the influence of Eastern philosophy on existentialism has been considerable. The denigration of mere rational or historical thought in contrast to living experience has its roots in Eastern religions.

Carl Gustav Jung too, the great Swiss psychiatrist, has made an impact not only on psychoanalysis and the practice of psychiatry, but also on religious thought. It would not be in place here to expound the religious thinking of Jung, but we need to note that Eastern religions played a significant role in forming his approach. He felt that Christians had much to learn from Hinduism and Buddhism, for he noted that the reality of the unconscious realm within humankind had been studied for two thousand years in the East and therefore 'doctrines have been developed which simply put all western attempts in the same line into the shade' (Jung's foreword to D. T. Suzuki: *An Introduction to Zen Buddhism* Grove, New York 1964). Jung felt that Western Christianity could get back in touch with the inner life through Zen Buddhism in particular.

In the contemporary world of theology, philosophy and psychology, Eastern religious thought makes a clear mark.

Some people may feel that the thinking of academics is irrelevant to the course of normal people's lives. This is far from the case. The deliberations of the ivory tower trickle gradually through into text books, college courses and the minds of teachers and lecturers at every level. In the next generation people take for granted what was previously the convoluted thought of the professors. So it is that the Eastern religious influence in previous academic circles has now begun to percolate through to the average student, Church member and to those still outside the Church.

iii) Why do Eastern religions appeal?
There seem to be two striking reasons why Eastern religions attract people in the West.

a) The failure of the Christian Church
Much of the worship and life of Western Churches appears rigid and formal, failing to satisfy the deeper spiritual nature in us all. Our worship services easily become a flood of words which sound magnificent but conceal the lack of intimate relationship and contact with the Lord himself. E. M. Forster's biting words 'poor little talkative Christianity' must surely apply to many of our services, which sometimes give the impression of being proficient stage-managed performances. Even the sermon can be so polished that it does not seem to come from the heart. My daughter once told me how much she had enjoyed a particular sermon because 'the preacher meant what he said'. I thought-lessly objected, but she innocently countered by stating firmly that preachers do not normally mean what they say. I would not wish to doubt the spiritual sincerity of most of the preachers my daughter had heard. However she did have a point. Perhaps

those preachers had not communicated in such a way that people knew that their words came with burning personal conviction.

In reaction against the rational and formal worship and teaching of the past some churches have developed new styles which can appear glib and superficial. In some churches I have noticed people praying with their hands in their pockets. This may symbolise their emphasis on the God who is lovingly intimate in his relationship with us and who welcomes us without the need for reverent forms of worship or prayer. The emphasis will be on the incarnate name 'Jesus' rather than 'Christ' or 'the Lord'. However, the biblical revelation shows us that our God is both burningly pure in his absolute holiness and also graciously accepting in his open-armed embrace of his children. In Colossians 1:15 Paul notes that God is still the one who is 'invisible', beyond all human description or knowledge. And yet at the same time we have in Jesus Christ the 'image' of the invisible God, so that we can know the unknowable, describe the indescribable, relate to him who is beyond all creation.

If the life, worship and preaching of the Church appears to lack a living spirituality, then people are going to look elsewhere. Formality, insincerity or a coldly cerebral approach will fail to meet the inner needs of our people. Likewise an unthinking emphasis on the heart without a sound biblical and theological use of the mind may lead to shallow worship which will also fail to satisfy. No wonder many are attracted by the apparently lively spirituality or deep mysticism of Hinduism and Buddhism.

The second reason hinges on the whole character of Western civilisation. We live in societies which depend on pressurised and competitive activity. Life moves fast. No longer can we stroll gently from place to place, but we rush with feverish desire to save time. When walking down a street or getting off a train, we all want to beat our neighbours and overtake them. I often notice this when travelling by plane. As soon as the plane has landed, people stand up to get their hand luggage and put on their coats. They eagerly await the opening of the doors so that they can rush off the plane. Actually it takes some time before the doors are opened and they will also have to wait for their luggage to get through. Although there is absolutely no purpose in their dedicated rush to move, Western culture pressurises us to get on with things as rapidly as possible.

But many people long to escape from the slavery of frenetic activity. The heart cries to the train of life, 'Stop! Let me get off!' Buddhist quietism seems to offer an attractive alternative to Western frenzy. The practice of yoga and transcendental meditation gives a real sense of peace. The Buddha's cool smile of non-emotion beckons the busy Westerner.

Is it then surprising that many today are asking questions related to Eastern religions? What sort of answers will the Christian Church give?

b) The global village

Just in the past few decades the countries of Europe have absorbed very large numbers of people from other countries. Many of these follow other religions – Islam, Hinduism, Buddhism, Judaism and Sikhism. While Germany has received many from Turkey and the former Yugoslavia, France has become the home for large numbers from North Africa. Britain has added to her population West Indians, Pakistanis, Bengalis and Sikhs particularly. Jews may be found in each of the European countries. More recently large numbers of Kurds and refugees from the former Yugoslavia and Afghanistan have swelled the numbers of Europe's ethnic minority populations.

While the first generation of immigrants tends to remain somewhat isolated from the native British, their children receive their education together with other British youngsters, speak English perfectly and usually mix relatively freely with their contemporaries. Some will have native English boyfriends or girlfriends, while a few will even marry out of their own racial community. The barriers begin to come down for some, but others have bad experiences of racialism and discrimination.

They may then become bitterly disillusioned with the host nation, feel themselves alienated and cut themselves off from relationships with people of a different race, colour or religion.

In Britain today we have about 1,250,000 Muslims, 300,000 registered Jews, 450,000 Sikhs, 450,000 Hindus and a considerable number of Buddhists, but statistics are not so easy to gather as Eastern religions do not form exclusive communities which can easily be numbered. Inter-racial and inter-religious relationships challenge the Church to prove whether its faith is authentic. Sadly the Church often retreats into a white ghetto. Christians rarely seem to know how to witness to ethnic communities around them, or even how to live as good neighbours among them. We desperately need help. Christians need to be encouraged, taught and trained. Our theological colleges have been slow to realise the primary importance of this in their training of the future leaders and ministers of the Church.

We now not only have large numbers of resident British Muslims, Jews and followers of Eastern religions, but we also receive many overseas visitors to our shores. Politicians, students, tourists and business people come here from all over the world and bring with them their own religions. Veiled women from the heartlands of Islam rub shoulders with scantily clad English girls in the London shops. Sikh turbans and beards sit next to white British youngsters in our universities.

As you walk the streets of any British city or major town you will be compelled to notice how varied the people around you are. The presence of other faiths in our midst forces itself upon us.

And these religions are not just passively present in our midst. They often rival or outdo the evangelistic zeal of the Christian Church. While it is true that the Jewish community does not seek to win converts and bitterly resents all Christian mission among them, Muslims, Hindus and Buddhists are often active in trying to win European converts to their faith. In some of our university or college campuses you are more likely to be given a Muslim tract than to meet Christian witness. Buddhists have set up several centres in order to attract British followers. And Hindu guru sects boldly witness on our streets. Particularly in the towns and cities British people may be compelled to give an answer. Mobile populations, ease of travel and mass communications bring the claims of other religions to our door, and we have to become aware that a rich variety of faiths all believe they have the truth. For some, another religion seems more attractive, or challenges previously held convictions.

Travel has now become both cheap and quick. When one reads of the long months spent by travellers in previous centuries on crowded sailing boats with inadequate food and hygiene, one realises how fortunate we are today. Even when my wife and I first went to Singapore as new missionaries it took us just over three weeks by ship. Now we can all fly anywhere in the world in a few hours. As a result, increasing numbers of Europeans travel all over the world and encounter other religions and their followers. Many are ill-equipped to face this challenge. Just today I received a letter from an Australian lady who had visited a strongly Muslim area of Indonesia. As a result she became bewildered and did not know how to relate her own Christian faith to the claims of Islam. She wrote to me because she had now just read a small book of mine, *Islam and Christian Witness*, which had apparently clarified her thinking.

Living not far from us is a former Pentecostal minister who spent some years working in South Yemen. He was impressed to see the local men praying five times daily and visiting the mosque for prayer while he was still in bed. He contrasted this with the lack of disciplined prayer in his church in England. As a result he came to feel that Islam is just as good a religion as Christianity. No longer could he preach about the unique glories of the atoning death and resurrection of Jesus Christ. He therefore resigned his ministry.

Recently a middle-aged couple shared their heartache. Their son had gone to Nepal on a visit, became attracted to the life of a Buddhist monastery there and now has disappeared leaving no trace of where he has gone to. They presume he must be living in some other monastery in Nepal.

c) Western cultural failure?

Christianity has often been closely associated with Western culture. Many people around the world assume that the Christian faith is a European or North American religion. In Malaysia I have often been told by local Chinese, 'I couldn't become a Christian, I'm Chinese.' There are obvious reasons for this misunderstanding, but of course the roots of Christianity lie in the Middle East. And from the beginning of the Church's history it spread across North Africa, east from Israel into West Asia, south into Ethiopia and across the Indian Ocean to India, probably through the apostle Thomas. Until the Crusades, the black African Nubian empire remained strongly Christian and the Thomas Christians in India have continued right through to today. In Europe itself the missionary endeavour battled against the heathen tribes of our continent for century after century until the last pagan community took the faith of Jesus Christ in the fourteenth century. In the village where I live there flows the river Lea, a small tributary of the Thames. Nine hundred years after Christ this river formed the boundary between Christian England and the pagan areas of the eastern parts of our island. A proper study of Church history actually negates the idea that Christianity is a Western religion. And certainly today the majority of Christians live in the southern hemisphere. Even in the Roman Catholic Church today the great majority of bishops are from the 'Third World'.

But still many in our Western Churches associate Christianity with Western culture. And we are going through a period of our history in which many are seriously questioning the value of European cultures. Because we doubt whether British culture is worth exporting, we begin also to doubt the unique validity of the Christian faith and therefore oppose any mission approach which attempts to convert people of other faiths. The failures of a European way of life raises doubts about the value of the Christian faith. Some ask whether the religions prevalent in other societies may not equally contain God's revelation.

With the followers of all the different faiths rubbing shoulders so closely these days, and with preconceptions and easily held certainties being challenged, it is inevitable that some will convert. Some Christians will leave their faith and follow another religion. Of course it may be equally true that more Muslims, Hindus or Buddhists may now become Christians. The doors are more open for movement from one religion to another than ever before in history.

Not only will people be converted from one religion to another, but we have to face the fact that other faiths now have considerable influence upon the thinking of our population. If our Christian witness is to be relevant, it must therefore tackle the question of other faiths and the Christian attitude to them.

2

Is There Revelation Outside
Jesus Christ and the Bible?

Without some form of revelation humankind cannot know the nature of God and his desires for us. We cannot know what is good and what is bad, what is truth and what falsehood. Without some form of revelation we sink in a quagmire of ignorance and uncertainty. Salvation then also becomes impossible.

That leads us to the topic for this chapter. How far can we say that revelation is to be found in the context of other non-Christian faiths? Or does God only reveal himself and his will through the incarnate and written Word of God, Jesus Christ and the Bible?

On this question Christian thinkers vary from the extreme view that all non-Christian religions represent demonic systems of untruth to the opposite extreme that they are all equally good. Woolly tolerance and vehement intolerance dismiss each other's views with equally confident disregard. Both sides run the danger of pride and intolerance. Both can fail to listen to the other and put their own views honestly under the careful scrutiny of God as revealed to us in Jesus Christ through the biblical scriptures.

1. Equally True?

A number of years ago an academic consultation on mission was held with participants from every continent and varied backgrounds, representing a wide range of theological positions. Most of the main addresses strongly advocated a universalistic approach, denying any belief in absolute truth with an arrogance and first-world imperialism. They therefore rejected the uniqueness of Christ as God incarnate and showed little interest in his atoning work on the cross for our sin. As the Roman Catholic L. Luzbetak says in *Catholic Evangelization Today* (ed. K. Boyack, Paulist Press 1987), 'The uniqueness, universality and finality of Jesus for all societies and cultures is, of course, unacceptable to not a few modern radical theologians.' Consequently on the question of revelation they would not countenance the uniqueness of Jesus Christ as the Word of God who shows us the Father in perfection. The Bible too would not be seen as God's revealed truth, but rather as a human book of deep religious insight. Both Jesus Christ and the Bible may be of significance for Christians, but they would deny any absolute claim over all humankind.

Perhaps the best-known name with respect to such views would be the Birmingham professor John Hick. He has written a book with Paul Knitter on the myth of the uniqueness of Christ. In his writings he inevitably has to face the question of revelation. In his book *Truth and Dialogue* he maintains that all religions and their inspired books are true for those who believe them. It is not that they have any objective or absolute truth inherent in them, but subjectively they become true as the believer accepts them. This parallels the Hindu parable of the snake which I have recounted before and which illustrates their philosophy of the various levels of truth.

So, likewise, Christ and the Bible contain truth for those who believe in them, but ultimately Hick would desire us to go beyond them to a higher absolute. He feels that all religions, their concepts of God and their apparently revealed scriptures are means towards 'the same ultimate divine reality'. None of them is a perfect revelation with any absolute truth. All theological theories or doctrines are merely ideas that 'men have developed to conceptualize the meaning of those encounters', those religious experiences of that ultimate divine reality. As in Hinduism so it seems with Hick the nature of this ultimate reality is quite vague. It cannot be defined as a personal God and it has no attributes or characteristics. Nor does it do anything. The traditional Christian might wish to dismiss it as an irrelevant and unprovable philosophical idea.

Strangely, Hick still affirms that Christ is *totus Deus*, 'wholly God', although not *totum Dei*, 'the whole of God'. He thus affirms that divine nature infuses the being of Christ (would he not also say the same of all human beings?), but rejects the biblical teaching that in Christ 'the whole fulness of deity dwells bodily' (Col. 2:9). No wonder then that Hick advocates that Christians should move beyond a Church-centred or a Christ-centred faith into a wider and less particularistic God-centred faith. Such a God-centred or Absolute-centred faith could include other religions and their 'revelations' as of equal validity.

One suspects that Hick owes much in his thinking to the writings of Wilfred Cantwell Smith, although he has developed Smith's thought considerably. As an Islamicist, Smith had a particular concern for the Muslim world, but this did not restrict his global vision. He stressed the reality of the one universal God and the community of all people – one God and one humanity. He saw religion as something which cuts people off from their natural relationship with God, but he also believed that all people can relate to God through their own religious traditions. Revelation is not narrow. It is not restricted to Jesus Christ and the Bible, but comes to all people within their own faith whether that be Christian, Muslim or Hindu. Like Hick, Smith concentrated his attention on the one God rather than on Jesus Christ as mediator between God and humanity. He is theocentric, not Christocentric. In that context he saw that all religions manifest unique reflections of the one Absolute, like the different colours in the rainbow together form a whole spectrum.

2. Liberation Theologies

Out of the heart-rending inequalities and injustices of the Latin American scene has come a rich stream of Christian thinkers who have related their faith to the pressing calls of their situation. The influence of liberation theology has spread beyond its original Roman Catholic boundaries into the Protestant churches and also into every continent. In the Latin American background these theologians hardly have to face the questions of relationship with other religions, for Latin America has relatively few Muslims, Hindus or Buddhists. But liberation theology implicitly relates to this question.

a) Biblical interpretation

Liberation theologians stress the importance of determining our religious faith and practice in the context of the socio-political situation in which we find ourselves. The founding father of liberation theology, Gustavo Gutierrez, emphasises that theology cannot be purely objective, but must flow out from our situation of oppression and lead to the right practice of justice. This has been thoroughly developed by J. L. Segundo in his *The Liberation of Theology*, where he shows the constant circle of biblical interpretation: injustice – theology – justice. The realities of injustice determine our understanding of theology which in turn leads us to right socio-political actions for justice.

This existential approach to biblical interpretation and to theology undermines a belief in objective, revealed truth. Justice, rather than truth, becomes the standard against which all is tested. All religions can accept that true religion requires justice, though we may debate the meaning and practical outworking of 'justice'.

In making truth of secondary importance, liberation theology opens the door to a tolerant universalism which may allow any religious belief as long as it works for justice.

b) Orthopraxis, not orthodoxy

Liberation theologians draw the inevitable conclusion from their situational approach to theology. They maintain that true religion consists in right practice rather than just right belief. This is a healthy reminder to traditional Christians that heresy is indeed not only wrong doctrine, but also the evil outworking of faith in practice. We have sometimes unduly emphasised doctrine to the neglect of good works. And our concept of good works has generally been restricted to the arena of our personal, private life rather than to the more public scene of the socio-political.

Swinging pendulums is a dangerous pursuit, however. Undue emphasis on doctrine to the neglect of righteousness and justice should not be remedied by overstressing the latter. Both in Judaism and biblical Christian thought faith and works should walk hand in hand. In Judaism it is hoped that the outward practice of good will influence us as people and form our character and thinking. In Christian thought our beliefs and our faith should produce the fruit of both personal and social righteousness. In both, however, truth is vital and must be manifest in right belief and right action. It is a sad reflection of human fallibility that Christian orthodoxy has so often failed to produce the desired justice and righteousness.

If we stress right practice rather than true doctrine, then there is no longer any division between those who believe in Jesus Christ and those who reject him. The division lies rather between those who practise justice and those who support the status quo. What religion you follow becomes much less important. So too Jesus Christ as the particular revelation of God can easily be underplayed and the absolute truth of the Bible as God's perfect word of objective truth is denied.

So we come again to the question as to whether true revelation is found in other religions. At this stage it may be helpful to look briefly at what some of the other major faiths say concerning revelation.

3. Concepts of Revelation in Other Religions

a) Judaism

Some Gentile Christians naïvely think of Judaism as purely the religion of the Old Testament. In fact its life and teachings are based also on the traditions of rabbinic study. Many Christians also fail to realise that Judaism, like Christianity, has divided into various separate groups. The main body is Orthodox Judaism, but Reform, Liberal and Reconstructionist synagogues all have their own theological beliefs and practices. More orthodox than the Orthodox are the Hasidim.

Many of the non-Orthodox Jews would deny that there is any absolute revelation, even in the Scriptures. They would revere the Bible as an inspired book hallowed by long centuries of Jewish tradition, but they would not consider it to be revelation direct from God himself. Inevitably they would not even consider the possibility of the Qur'an, New Testament or other religious books being absolute revealed truth. But just like more liberal Christians who deny that the Bible is God's revealed word, so also such Jews may tend to be quite tolerant of other religions as being valid ways for Gentiles to come towards God. They would not claim for themselves any exclusive revelation of truth.

For Orthodox Jews the situation is different. They believe that the Torah, the Law, is written by God and revealed to Israel through Moses. It is channelled through Moses, but he does not impart to its contents anything of his own personality or historical situation. The Torah is absolute God-given revelation.

But then we have to ask what the Torah consists of. In concentric circles it widens out from the Ten Commandments to the five books of Moses, the Pentateuch. It then includes the whole Tenach, which Christians call the Old Testament. This is the 'written Torah'. But Orthodox Jews believe also in 'oral Torah'. That consists primarily of the Talmud, but then also includes all the traditions of rabbinic studies. Officially oral Torah is a never-ending revelation which embraces whatever a recognised orthodox rabbi states in answer to a question from one of his people. All oral Torah is said to come from God and to have been revealed through Moses, but not written down. It is then brought to the notice of Israel through the succession of rabbis through the centuries.

Written and oral Torah together contain God's full and absolute revealed truth for Israel. No other religion's holy books in any way parallel Torah. Some Orthodox Jews may recognise that the New Testament, the Qur'an and other books have some truth which may be of use to Gentiles in their religious life, but these books are in no way God's revealed word.

Is the Torah only for Jews or also for all humankind? In the Torah we have the pre-Abrahamic Law of Noah which has universal validity. In it God reveals his fundamental demands for all people. In Torah we are also given the revelation of the character of God himself. This is of course an objective revelation of God's nature which will always be just as true for Gentiles as for Jews. But the heart of the Torah is the Mosaic Law which God gave to Israel and is only for Israel. Other religious systems may be good for Gentiles, but ultimately it has to be said that they are missing God's best, his full revelation. They may enter into this revelation by joining themselves to Israel as proselytes and there is a long history of Jewish endeavours to encourage others to follow God's revealed Law.

b) Islam

Like Orthodox Judaism, Islam too has a strong doctrine of revelation. The Qur'an is said to have been written by God on a tablet in heaven before all time. Just as Christians have tried to marry the timeless eternity of Christ with the fact that the Father is the origin of all, so likewise Muslim theology has affirmed that the Qur'an is uncreated and eternal, but that it was written by God. Christians say that Christ was 'begotten' of the Father, but not created. Muslims parallel this in stating that the Qur'an was 'written' by God, but not created.

Christians believe that the Bible is God's revealed word and yet at the same time we claim that it was written by men whose personality and historical circumstances affect the content of their writings. So it would be inconceivable that Luke could have written the book of Jeremiah or vice versa. They spoke different languages. They lived at different periods of history and this shapes their message. Luke was a doctor, so very interested in Jesus' miracles and how they took place. Jeremiah was somewhat depressive, so bemoaned his calling as a prophet. So the writers play a formative part in passing on God's word. In Islam this is not the case. God wrote the Qur'an before history. The Qur'an was merely channelled through the Prophet. Muslims have therefore traditionally affirmed that Mohammed was illiterate and so could not possibly have written the Qur'an with all its beauty and wisdom. Because the Qur'an is seen as God's own writing with no human influence, Muslims can never dissect and criticise it like Christians have done to their Bible. God's word may only be revered and obeyed. There can be no debate as to whether parts of it are culturally determined in some way.

In addition to the Qur'an, Islam reveres the collections of Mohammed's words, deeds and thoughts. These collections are called 'hadith'. They too come from God, but obviously the man Mohammed has played a vital part in forming their content. No Muslim doubts the authority of genuine hadith as revealing the will of God. Nevertheless the hadith stand somewhat below the Qur'an on the ladder of revelation.

Like every other religion Islam too has a variety of different denominations. These may also hold varying views concerning revelation. So Shi'i Islam, whose heartland lies in Iran, underlines the uniqueness of Qur'anic revelation, but then adds to it. The direct successors of Mohammed may have a divine authority of applying the teachings of the Qur'an. So the very title 'ayatollah' is significant – the sign or verse of God. These descendants of Mohammed channel the revealed word of God to the people. Their word becomes God's word. The mystic Sufis on the other hand stress above all experience of God as the supreme way of revelation. This can lead to a universalist tolerance of other mystical ways to the one God.

Mohammed stressed in his teaching that his revelations stood directly in the succession of previous prophets and holy books. He saw himself as reiterating the message of Abraham, Moses, David, Jesus and all the great earlier prophets. Islam believes there have been four great books which God has written and revealed through his prophets. The Taurat or Law came through Moses, the Zabur or Psalms through David, the Injil or Gospel through Jesus and finally the Qur'an through the last and greatest prophet, Mohammed. In theory then Muslims believe in the Jewish and Christian Scriptures, but the Qur'an accuses us of having corrupted and mislaid the revelations of God. The Bible we now have is therefore considered to be a man-made falsification of the books which God wrote in heaven.

How then do Muslims view other religions and their holy books? The answer for orthodox Sunni Muslims is clear. There is one God, one final prophet, Mohammed, and one perfect revealed word from God, the Qur'an. All humankind must submit to Allah, Mohammed and the Qur'an. The very words 'Islam' and 'Muslim' come from an Arabic root meaning 'submit'.

What then is the Christian response to the claims of Islam? How does the Christian view the Muslim belief that the Qur'an is absolutely the word and words of God revealed miraculously to and through Mohammed? What was happening when Mohammed was in the cave receiving his revelations from the heavenly archangel?

Christians respond to these questions with a whole spectrum of attitudes. The Roman Catholic theologian Hans Kung *(Christianity and the World Religions)* at least suggests the possibility that Mohammed was indeed a prophet and that the Qur'an parallels the Old Testament as an inspired word from God. At the other end of the theological spectrum, conservative scholars like John Gilchrist would consider the Qur'an to be inspired not by God, but rather by Satan. In its demonic falsehood it deceives Muslims, hardening them against the truth in Jesus Christ. We may suggest a *via media* in which truth is sadly perverted, but there remain elements both of truth and falsehood. Might it be that God spoke to Mohammed and called him to bring the Arabs away from idolatrous animism to the worship of the one true God? Might it then be that Mohammed distorted God's call, misunderstood and rejected the Christian faith – perhaps also because the Church has often presented a false witness? But there remains much that is true within Islam, although that truth is corrupted and used by Satan to blind people to the glories of life and salvation through Jesus Christ.

c) Hinduism

We now move from the more familiar Jewish–Christian–Muslim religion into the totally different sphere of Eastern religious philosophies, mysticism and myth. In non-dualistic Hinduism nothing has a separate existence, for ultimately only the Absolute Brahman is. In our ignorance we may think that we are, but actually we too are Brahman. No dualism of I–Thou or Brahman-creation can be allowed. One might therefore feel that this major school of Hinduism could not countenance any idea of revelation, as G. Parrinder rightly observes in his *Avatar and Incarnation*:'For religious life some kind of objective relationship with a deity seems to be necessary.' The very idea of revelation demands that there be a revealer and somebody to whom he or it reveals.

There is however another major stream of Hinduism which does allow dualism. Here the non-personal Brahman also has a personal aspect which can be incarnated on earth and relate to human beings. These avatar or incarnations include such beings as the black and beautiful Krishna. Parrinder calls Krishna 'the revealed God' and says, 'The Lord takes human form through compassion to make himself understandable to his followers.'

Parrinder not only notes the concept of revelation in the incarnations of Brahman, but also supremely in the Hindu classics, 'The Scriptures are there telling us what Brahman is, and nowhere else do we find it.' But the Vedas themselves in the 'Hymn to the Unknown God' underline the impossibility of knowing who or what the 'creative force' is or how this world came into being.

In Hindu philosophy a distinction is made between *sruti* and *smrti*. *Sruti* contains the idea of something that is heard, for it is believed that the Vedas were heard direct from above by the *rishis* or seers. As in the Bible there is the double emphasis that the word of revelation is both heard and seen – it is heard by seers. *Smrti*, on the other hand, is that which is remembered by people. That which is heard depends on what human beings remember and the two come to coincide. So dualist and non-dualist philosophies come together in affirming that knowledge from outside ourselves is dependent on an awareness from within. Indeed in Hinduism it is impossible to distinguish between objective revelation and subjective intuition or consciousness.

This traditional emphasis on the subjective is taken considerably further in the philosophy of Professor Radhakrishnan, the former president of India and the immensely influential Hindu thinker and writer. In his *Religion in a Changing World* he stresses that no revelation by a book or by an incarnation can be fully true, for all is relative. He states that, 'The only thing that is finally valid is the inner experience of the Absolute.'

All truth is relative – all knowledge is subjective – subjective experience is more important than historical facts – the Absolute is unknowable and indescribable, neither personal nor impersonal. Such statements have influenced the Western world and crept into some forms of Christian theology too. Inevitably they undermine any belief in Jesus Christ as the final and absolute revelation of God according to the Scriptures. And if all truth is relative and subjective, no so-called revelation can be complete or perfect. The only absolute truth is that there is no knowable absolute truth. Such a philosophy must lead to a tremendous tolerance of all other philosophies as long as they do not believe in any absolute, particularistic or exclusive truth. It is tolerant of tolerance, but firmly intolerant of any assured faith in a revealed or absolute truth.

d) Buddhism

Can there be any form of revelation in Buddhism? Without a belief in any absolute being or power Buddhism would seem to deny the possibility of a doctrine of revelation. Ultimately Buddhism not only rejects the concept of any divine being who might be the revealer, but also holds to the doctrine of *Anatta*, 'No-Self'. If in Hinduism we have finally to say that nothing exists except Brahman, in Buddhism nothing exists. So in the last analysis there is nobody to whom revelation might be granted. A famous Buddhist scripture states:

> Mere suffering exists, no sufferer is found;
> The deed is, but no doer of the deed is there;
> Nirvana is, but not the man that enters it;
> The Path is, but no traveller on it is seen.
> *Visuddhi Magga xvi*

Such a doctrine leads to an easy tolerance of other faiths and their followers, for in theory Buddhism does not believe anything, anybody or any faith has ultimate existence. Everything is an illusion.

But in practice there is another side of Buddhism. The Buddha himself preached the Buddhist way and thus set the wheel of its teaching in motion. As Peter Masefield convincingly demonstrates in his *Divine Revelation in Pali Buddhism*, people may enter the path towards enlightenment by hearing the dharma, the teaching of the Buddha. Conversion therefore comes from a right hearing of the dharma, leading to a right view of life. Although Walpole Rahula★ denies the possibility of grace in Buddhist philosophy, Masefield shows grace can come through hearing the word of the Buddha.

The Buddha's word may come to us in two ways. Firstly it is mediated through his recorded teachings in the Buddhist scriptures. Critics may severely question how much of the scriptures actually originates from the Buddha himself, but at least we may say that they spring from the source of his teaching. Secondly, Masefield suggests that grace and full enlightenment can only come from direct hearing of the teaching from the actual lips of the Buddha himself. There can therefore be no revelation or enlightenment after the death of the Buddha until his coming again in his final reincarnation as Maitreya Buddha. Meanwhile all Buddhists seek to earn adequate merit in order to be ready for grace through the teachings of Maitreya Buddha.

In Christianity, God primarily reveals his own nature and thus the way of reconciliation with him. In Judaism and Islam, God primarily reveals his will, but not so much his nature. Except in mystical Sufism, Islam sees God as utterly distinct from humankind and the Creation, so that God in his person becomes ineffably high and almost unknowable. In Hinduism the personalised form of Brahman seeks to reveal the nature of the cosmos. In Buddhism the Buddha reveals the way of enlightenment in which one moves beyond the state of existence into the great void where there is neither being nor non-being. Of course these summaries of the content of revelation are over-simplified,

---

★cf. *Buddhist Studies in Honour of I. B. Horner*, ed. L. Cousins, Dordrecht 1974

but they nevertheless indicate the basic thrust of each. They may differ in the aim and form of their revelations, but all claim to give their followers the truth.

What then as biblical Christians should we say about revelation? Can we allow that truth may lie also in these other faiths or does God only reveal himself and his ways in Jesus Christ and the Bible?

4. General Revelation

As we have already seen, the Bible makes it clear that some knowledge of God may be found without his specific self-revelation in Jesus Christ and in his written word. Romans 1 and 2 show that God reveals himself in nature and through the human conscience. But we should also observe that such divine revelation does not preclude the necessity of God's saving work in Christ, for sin continues to pervert human nature and our understanding of God's truth.

Jung rightly observed this subjective reflection of God which lies deep within the unconscious of us all. He felt that within every human being is found the image of God. Actually the Bible says more than that. It is not only that the image of God is within our unconscious, but rather that the totality of our being is created in God's image and likeness. The image of God is not just seen in human dominion over nature or in any morally God-like righteousness, as some have maintained. Nor does the image of God merely reflect our immortality or the Trinitarian nature of God in our memory, intelligence and will (cf. Augustine: *De Trinitate*). The whole of us, both individually and in our social and ecological relationships, reflects the total nature and being of God. Although sin has sadly perverted this original image of God in which we were created, yet to some extent it remains as a vital aspect of human nature. As human beings we are like a crooked mirror which reflects and at the same time distorts the image of God. Only Jesus Christ is without sin and therefore perfectly 'reflects the glory of God and bears the very stamp of his nature' (Heb. 1:3). Jesus can say 'He who has seen me has seen the Father' (John 14:9).

Because of the very nature of humankind as a distorted image of God, it is natural for us all to search for something religious in life. Even the supposedly atheist Communist countries have found it necessary to produce religious substitutes for their people – pictures of the nation's leader to revere, semi-religious wedding and funeral services, the near deification of the founding fathers, Marx and Lenin.

In other parts of the world, humankind has developed a wide variety of religious forms and faiths. Each nation and people struggles to express their fundamental beliefs in a Creator God and discovers ways to serve and worship him. So the Kenyan theologian John Mbiti calls the traditional African tribal religions 'one scene of man's groping after his Creator'. While the Christian will not hesitate to accept that other faiths contain a mixture of general revelation and human searching for God, we may also want to affirm that religion can also obscure any true knowledge of God. Religion, be it Christian or non-Christian, contains two elements simultaneously. It can reflect the human search for God which is part of our natural created humanness. But at the same time religion may be a means by which we push God away from us and avoid any vital encounter with God. It is difficult to concur with more definite claims to objective supernatural revelation in Islam, Hinduism or Buddhism. Even Hans Kung hesitates to accept that the Qur'an was written by God in heaven without human participation, although with customary tolerance he does want to agree that it is God's revealed word.

5. God's Word

While it is true that God does reveal himself and his will in human nature and through all of his Creation, these forms of revelation remain inadequate. The Bible makes it clear that God also loves to speak to his people by words and works. It is sometimes said that in the Bible God speaks through his actions in history, but his direct words communicate even more definitely.

In today's world we have come to despise words as mere verbiage. We have become disillusioned with political double-talk in the affairs both of Church and State. Slick slogans have therefore been coined: 'actions speak louder than words' or 'your life shouts so loudly I can't hear your words'. But actually your actions and your life fail to communicate at all adequately if they are not accompanied and explained by words. This is true also of God's dynamic actions in history; they too need words. The miracles of Jesus and the apostles were sensational, but without the preached word no one knew what they really meant. Such outward signs as the covenant rainbow in Noah's time or the Last Supper bread and wine could never be understood without some accompanying verbal explanation. Still today many non-Christians gaze admiringly at a rainbow, but they do not think of God's promises to humankind after the Flood.

So God speaks supremely through words. The Bible tells how this world started with God's spoken word. God said, ' "Let there be light" ' (Genesis 1:3). And his word contained such power that Creation came into being. John's Gospel picks up this theme in saying that all things were made through the Word (John 1:3). Then again and again throughout the history of God's people in the Old Testament we read how God spoke directly to them. As a result the prophets were able to affirm confidently 'thus says the Lord'. They knew that their words were actually the very words of God himself. So the Bible makes it clear that God's words create and communicate.

Then in the New Testament God's creative word came into the world, took flesh and dwelt among us (John 1:9,14). As the writer to the Hebrews says, 'In many and various ways God spoke of old to our fathers by the prophets; but in these last days he has spoken to us by a Son' (Heb. 1:1,2). God not only speaks to us through his words in the Bible, but also more perfectly still in his incarnate word, Jesus Christ himself. The Bible as well as all the revelations claimed in other religions merely acts as a signpost to show us the way to God. Jesus is himself the way. We not only discover the way to God through him, but we also find God *in* him for he *is* God. He not only reveals; he is the revelation.

6. Christian Arrogance?

Theologians like Paul Knitter, John Hick and Hans Kung confidently assert that such an assured faith in God's revelation in Christ as the unique, absolute truth can only lead to arrogant intolerance. Thus Kung comments that, 'Absolute truth becomes tolerant only when people no longer believe in it.'

If indeed God has spoken to us with an objective word from himself, then that revelation must be the yardstick by which we assess everything. If therefore we believe that the Bible is God's written word and that Jesus Christ is the word of God incarnate, then we can only affirm that God's word is the criterion for judging all other claims to truth.

But do we then become arrogantly intolerant? Surely not. If indeed we believe that we have assured objective truth by God's revelation rather than through our own intelligence or spiritual acumen, we have no cause for pride. We are merely stewards of God's revelation and truth which he has graciously given to us. Arrogance may actually prove more of a temptation to those who reject the absolute truth of God's revealed word and therefore have to rely on their own understanding of religious reality. Although the word of God is absolutely perfect, we are deeply aware that our understanding of that word remains imperfect. We also know that we have much to learn about how to live out God's will. We continue to fall far short of his standards. Because we believe that all human beings and all religious faiths retain something of God's image and truth, we know that we can learn from other faiths and their followers. They may often rebuke us for our disobedience to God's word and show us where we have failed to grasp all that his word contains. Even though we have been redeemed by the grace of God active in the death and resurrection of Christ, as sinners we should never entertain the temptation to be proud. An assured faith in God's revelation of himself in the Bible and in Jesus Christ can and should co-exist with gracious humility. We confess our failure always to achieve that humility, but nevertheless reject Kung's statement that a standpoint of exclusivity or of superiority can only lead to 'comfortable apologetics, to a closed and opinionated mind, in short to the dogmatism which thinks it already possesses the whole truth'. We do have the whole truth in God's written and incarnate word, but we need to grow in our understanding and practice of that truth. Sin and blindness cling to us, but we look to the Holy Spirit to go on teaching and sanctifying.

3

Who Is God?
A Variety of Answers

In the last chapter we discussed different approaches to the question of revelation. Although we observed that not all religions believe that it is God himself who is revealed, biblical faith is centred on the revelation of the person of God. So now in this chapter we shall look at what the major world faiths believe about God. Of course they will not all use the word 'God', for not all believe in a personal deity. But each faith has a belief in some ultimate reality or power. Then it has to be said too that each faith has its own understanding of the character and nature of that ultimate being.

Not only do different faiths have varying understandings of God's nature, but actually every individual human being may have their own concept of God. It would be interesting to ask a random selection of men and women in the street how they picture God and what he is like. I am sure that even in nominally Christian societies the answers would vary considerably. Although they might all use the name 'God', their understanding of him might not fit how the Bible describes him.

So now let us examine briefly what the major religions of the world have to say about God or whatever supreme power rules in their faith.

1. Tribal Religions

In a series of books Don Richardson has developed the earlier research of Father Schmidt in showing that all peoples originally believed in a High God who created the universe. Richardson seems to be a little weak in his evidence when talking about some of the Asian religions, but generally it would seem that his point is valid. In early Chinese religion Shang Ti prefigured later ideas of heaven as the founder of the world and all people. In Indian religions there is not only the great impersonal Brahman, but in the earlier forms of Indian religion the pantheon of gods was headed by Surya, the Sun God, the author of life and birth. Surya was the supreme deity who seems later to have merged with Vishnu, the personalised form of Brahman. Some scholars have suggested however that Surya was merely the eye of Varuna, the Sky God, who created all things and governs the universe. A third candidate for the position of supreme deity was Indra, from whom all other deities were said to come. Indra was known as the bull which united with the cosmic cow goddess to give birth to the universe. While these myths have lost any clear indication of which deity was the original supreme creator, the mists of time have not dimmed the fact that early Indian religion did believe in one creator God.

The same may be said for all tribal religions. My wife and I worked for some years among the Karo Batak people in North Sumatra, Indonesia. Like each of the five Batak peoples, the Karo Batak believed in a great creator God called Dibata. Dibata was manifest in three aspects. 'Dibata above' had power over all things above the earth – the sun, moon, stars, clouds, wind and rain. 'Dibata in the middle' ruled over the surface of the world – fields, rivers, mountains and all that grows. 'Dibata below' lay beneath the surface of the world's crust, but emerged mysteriously and frighteningly in the local volcanoes and hot springs.

Such beliefs could be paralleled in the traditions of tribes in every continent. Missionaries and anthropologists all over the world have researched such ancient religious beliefs and there can be little doubt that all hold a common faith in one high creator God.

But what is this High God like?

Generally speaking, the tribal High God tends to be thought of as a personal deity, but remote and distant from humankind. Because the High God is so difficult to reach, people often concentrate their prayer and worship on lesser deities or spirits. These may be worshipped in idol forms or at special shrines. For example the ancient Anglo-Saxon peoples seem to have believed in a High Creator whom they called 'God', but much of their religious life centred on such lesser deities as Thor and Wodun. It is of course significant for modern mission that the name 'God' was happily taken over for the Hebrew 'Elohim' and the Greek 'Theos', but Thor, Wodun and the other lesser deities were anathema to the new Christian faith.

In the Old Testament the Creator is called Elohim in the early chapters of Genesis. But then in Genesis 14 the strange and heathen character of Melchizedek advances on to the stage of biblical history. He introduces 'El' to the people of God. El was the creator deity worshipped by the majority of Middle Eastern peoples, including the Canaanites and Philistines. This pagan name for the Creator thus became entirely equivalent to Eloah and the plural Elohim. But any untrue understandings of his nature or the way he works had to be changed to fit in with the biblical revelation. Likewise when Israel was exiled to Babylon they found that the people there worshipped Elah as the creator deity and this name was also adopted into biblical revelation. It first appears in the Bible in the book of Ezra. Again we note that Elah becomes interchangable with Elohim or El. The Babylonians' heathen understanding of the nature of Elah needed of course to be corrected in the light of the scriptures and of Israel's experience of El/Elohim. In the Jewish Septuagint and the New Testament the Greek word 'Theos' is likewise adopted into the Jewish and Christian faiths, but again the understanding of his nature and way of working is adapted and corrected. So it is biblical to take over non-Christian creator deities and their names as long as non-Christian misunder-standings are not allowed to creep into the Christian faith.

On the other hand it should be noted that the Old Testament vehemently opposes all compromise with shrine deities or idols. The Baalim and their shrines are to be destroyed. Politically correct tolerance is anathema in relation to all idols and to the Baalim. In the New Testament also the personalised idol deities are opposed tooth and nail. There can be no question of relating Elohim or YHWH to Mercury, Diana or other such deities. The same principle applies to early Christian mission in Europe. The Pagan creator deities of God, Gott, Dieu, Dios or the Slavonic Bog are accepted into the Christian faith with biblical adaptation, but the lower level idol figures such as Thor or Wodun are totally rejected. Strangely they remain in the names for the days of the week, but religiously they were cast out. Today too in our mission worldwide we follow this same pattern of accepting the creator High God, but rejecting all idols and shrine gods or spirits.

Much has been written about African tribal religions and their belief in a High God. For example John Mbiti from Kenya in his *Concepts of God in Africa* combines the beliefs of many different tribes all over the continent to show that many biblical descriptions of God can be paralleled in African tribal religions. He further shows that the High God's activities relate closely to the works of God in the Bible. We may criticise his book for its failure adequately to consider the corruption of truth in African religions and for the way he pools insights from a multitude of tribes as if they formed one faith. Nevertheless we can see that much of the nature and working of God may be discovered by people outside of the direct and full revelation in Jesus Christ and the Bible. But, as we have noted, such knowledge will need to be corrected and filled out by the perfect revelation of God in his word.

2. Islam

The Arabs at the time of Mohammed consisted of many tribal groups whose religion manifested the same characteristics as in other tribal faiths around the world. Above all there reigned the High God Allah who created the world. But Allah remained high above all human reach, so normal worship was concentrated on some lower deities whose shrines happened to be in the district of Mecca where Mohammed was born and brought up. These lesser gods were thought to be the daughters of Allah, named Allat, Al–Manat and Al–Uzza. Some scholars suggest that Allat may have been the wife rather than the daughter of Allah. Just as the early missionaries to Europe took over and refined the local belief in 'God' but totally rejected the lesser deities of Thor and Wodun, so too Mohammed retained Allah but destroyed the shrines of his daughters and forbade their worship.

So Islam came to emphasise faith in the one unique Creator God. In so doing it has strongly rejected any duality in the oneness of God, thus outlawing any approach to the Christian faith in the Trinity. In the context of Allah's daughters it is also not surprising to read the Qur'an's vehement opposition to the idea that God might have a son.

But the traditional pre-Muslim Arab view of Allah relegated Allah to a remote distance from humankind. Without a Trinitarian view of God which allows him to remain in distant glory while also descending to earth in incarnate form, Islam has found it difficult to maintain the distinct otherness and greatness of Allah and yet at the same time bring him within human reach. It is true that in theory Islam has tempered the otherness of Allah with the traditional belief that he is nearer to us than our neck artery, but in practice orthodox Islam has considered God to be virtually unknowable. In contrast to the Christian emphasis on knowing, loving and being united with God, orthodox Islam rather stresses the believers' duty to submit in obedience to Allah. The very words 'Islam' and 'Muslim' signify submission.

The key to the Muslim understanding of the nature of Allah is then twofold. He is one and he is supremely great.

In comparative religious studies it is possible to list all the basic characteristics of God in Islam and Christianity. Superficially they may appear to be very similar. Both believe God to be all-powerful, merciful (the Christian might prefer the word 'loving'), holy, omniscient, etc. But the ranking of these various characteristics is in a significantly different order. While almost every chapter of the Qur'an is headed with an ascription to God the merciful, yet God's mercy is inseparably related to and beneath his sovereign power.

Christians too believe that God's sovereign power reigns over the world he has made. But we believe that the use of this power is tempered by God's holiness and gracious humility as seen in his son, Jesus Christ. The Christian faith depends on the affirmation that God must do what is right and loving, while he cannot do what is unholy or unloving. In his humility God has limited the exercise of his almighty power to fit his holiness and love. So the Christian can know with assurance that God must keep his promises in his word. He will only do what is right and true.

In orthodox Islam Allah is not emotionally involved with his people or his creation, but in his majestic greatness demands obedient submission. In Muslim traditions therefore God says, 'These to heaven and I care not; these to hell and I care not.' To the Christian such a statement from God would be impossible, for God does care. And his judgments are always given with absolute holiness, not by arbitrary whim. But Allah can do anything according to his own will.

Bible concordances contain long columns of references to the holiness of God and also to God's requirement that we too should be holy. In Islam much emphasis is put on the so-called ninety-nine most beautiful names of Allah. In most Muslim societies men finger the beads of their rosaries to remind them of those names. But only one name refers to God as holy. It is not a common theme of the Qur'an at all.

So the key to understanding the Muslim view of Allah is the common declaration that God is the greatest, Allahu Akbar, and so can do whatever he wills. God may indeed show mercy to those who do good and follow him, but his mercy does not stem from the absolute demands of his righteousness nor from a loving heart. As Hasan Askari (quoted in K. Cragg's *The Pen and the Faith*) has written, 'God is not delighted by obedience, nor displeased by sins, nor merciful to the believer, nor disgusted with the forgetful . . . nor hostile to the arrogant. He is above all associations.'

How then does the Christian react to the Muslim belief in Allah? When the Muslim declares that God is one, the Christian delights to reply 'Amen'. In Islam the opposite of God's oneness is the major sin of Shirk, associating something or someone with God. So Muslims react strongly against the Christian doctrine of Christ which puts him in association with God the Father. If Jesus were not God, then it would indeed constitute an idolatrous denial of God's uniqueness. But the Christian affirms that this unique oneness is manifested in the three persons of the Trinity. When the Qur'an underlines the mercy of God, the Christian rejoices to share this great reality with Muslim friends. But we want to add that this mercy is based on the unchanging love of God.

While agreeing that God delights to show mercy to his people, Christians rejoice that we can move beyond the Muslim concept of mercy to the biblical assurance of grace. While the Qur'an maintains that mercy is exercised towards those 'who do good', grace is the undeserved love of God for sinners. Muslims find real difficulty in understanding how Jesus could promise the repentant thief on the cross that he would that very day be with

Jesus in paradise. To the Muslim this seems utterly unjust, for the thief was an evil man who had no further time or opportunity for amassing sufficient compensating good works. Jesus' words sound grossly unjust therefore to a Muslim. In their eyes God's mercy is only shown towards those who submit to the will of God and follow him in obedience. The glorious truth of God's grace may include the Muslim idea of mercy, but it goes far beyond it.

When the world of Islam defiantly proclaims that Allah is the greatest, again the Christian is reminded of our faith in the almighty God. But we remember too the words of the Creed, 'I believe in God the Father Almighty.' The all-powerful God is also our loving heavenly Father. And we are his children. So to the Christian the affirmation that God is the greatest is not a proudly defiant or aggressive statement. Rather it strikes a note of confident faith in our loving Father. And we know that God's total holiness keeps the exercise of God's power within the limits of truth, justice and grace.

So as Christians we delight to acknowledge many areas of agreement with Muslims about the nature of God, but at the same time we have to face the fact that in our witness we shall want to introduce new elements into the Muslim understanding of Allah. We shall also need to adjust misunderstandings of Allah in the light of Jesus Christ and the biblical revelation.

3. Judaism

With their common background of the Old Testament it might at first sight appear self-evident that Christianity and Judaism would have the same understanding of the nature of God. But we always need to remind ourselves that the common Old Testament roots have branched out in different directions. Judaism has developed a long history of rabbinic teaching, while Christianity has understood the Old Testament in the light of Jesus as Messiah and the New Testament's interpretation of all previous revelation. Inevitably therefore we find considerable areas of agreement between the two faiths, but also some clashes.

As with Islam, so also Judaism has found the Christian belief in the Trinity an insurmountable stumbling-block. With their strict background of faith in the oneness of God, the first disciples of Jesus must also have found it hard to reconcile the unity of God with their growing awareness of Jesus' deity and then of the Holy Spirit as God. Indeed it took several centuries and much argument before the Church actually formulated its Trinitarian theology in credal form. But Judaism has never been able to follow that path. It firmly rejected the deity of Jesus and built its faith immovably on the unity of God.

Largely through the great twelfth-century Jewish philosopher and theologian Moses Maimonides, the Jewish doctrine of God's oneness was subtly changed. The biblical affirmation that 'God is one' uses a Hebrew word for 'one' which may allow diversity within the unity. Maimonides in his famous Thirteen Principles slightly alters this, thus forming a word for 'one' which disallows any diversity within the unity of God. In this way he purposely excludes the Christian faith from being at all accepted by Orthodox Jews. To Christian Jews this is sad, for we would love Orthodox Jews to recognise that Christianity is in fact a Jewish faith at heart, but which is universal and open to all races.

While Judaism strongly recognises the reality of sin and evil, it has not believed in a personal Devil as the origin of all evil. When this is linked to the biblical truth that God is above all and the source of all, it can lead to an undue emphasis on the dark side of God. God becomes the cause of tragedy and sin as well as the one who gives all good gifts. Jewish films and books constantly bring out this aspect of Jewish faith. Persecution and trauma are also the result of God's work, not just an evil which the sovereign God may permit. In the minds of most Jews, God becomes somewhat unpredictable. He may give us what is good, but he may also show a vindictive or malignant streak which is frightening. For some reason he may decide to send a plague or a pogrom on his people. Many Jews feel dangerously vulnerable as God's chosen people. Gentile Christians may enviously declare that it must be wonderful to be Jewish, but Jews themselves do not share that feeling. Being Jewish causes problems, not least with God himself. Judaism allows us no assurance in God's steadfast love in practice, for as the source of good and evil one can never be sure what he will do. While we also reject an unbiblical dualism in which God and Satan are two eternal equally powerful foes, the common Jewish failure to believe in a personal Devil leads to a wrong view of God.

In secular Western Gentile society New Age occultism and contemporary European pagan cults have revived an interest in evil spirits and the person of Satan. But generally the Devil has been discredited as an obsolete and ridiculous personification of evil. In a blame culture however someone has to carry the can for life's tragedies. So God is commonly blamed for wars, sickness and natural disasters. Crime and the heartaches of broken relationships are seen as the consequence of poverty and social exclusion. Satan and sin are ignored as the fundamental origin of all evil. Western societies desperately need to recover the Christian understanding not only of Satan, but also of the positive holiness of God. He may be sovereign over all, but all evil should be laid firmly at the door of Satan working in and through a fallen creation and the sin of human beings

As with Islam, so with Judaism the lack of Trinitarian faith causes many problems. It is through the knowledge of God incarnate as a human being that Christians know the reality of a God of glory and yet also of gracious humility. In Jesus Christ we see God's absolutely trustworthy love. He never does anything evil or unloving. Without such knowledge of Jesus Christ as the revelation of the nature of God it is almost impossible to grasp the fullness of his perfection. This is sadly evident both in Islam and Judaism.

4. Hinduism

'African tribal religions believe . . .'; 'Islam believes . . .'; 'Judaism holds that . . .' Such statements may overgeneralise, for actually no religion is monolithic. Each has a variety of movements or denominations which will teach differently both about revelation and about the nature of God. If this is true of tribal religions, Islam and Judaism, it is doubly so in Hinduism. In his Penguin book on Hinduism, K. C. Sen rightly points out that, 'The religious beliefs and practices of different schools of Hindu thought differ; there is in it monism, dualism, monotheism, polytheism, pantheism.' In my lectures to students on this topic I always point out that whatever I say may be contradicted by some other school of Hindu philosophy. The scholar struggles to get a grasp of Hinduism, but finds it is like fighting with an octopus. There is always another tentacle to attack one unexpectedly from behind.

It may appear over-simplified, but it remains helpful to divide Hindu philosophy into two main groups – dualist and non-dualist or advaitin.

a) Advaitin – non-dualist

We have previously observed that in this form of Hinduism only Brahman ultimately is. All else is an illusion, for all is really Brahman. In the Vishnu Purana it is said, 'In truth, the world is He.' The classic scriptures contain many descriptions of Brahman while at the same time maintaining that he or it is beyond all description except through negatives. Perhaps the best-known pair of expressions of the reality of Brahman is *Tat Sat* and *Na iti, na iti*. The former means 'It Is' and demonstrates that Brahman is the unique ultimate reality. The world is merely his or its plaything which originated from Brahman and exists because of his sustaining. But while Brahman may be defined as *Tat Sat*, actually Brahman is truly *Na iti, na iti* which means 'Not this, not this'. I have used the words 'he' and 'it' for Brahman, but

Brahman is neither personal nor impersonal. Brahman is indescribable. Whatever one says about him or it, the answer returns 'Not this, not this'. The ultimate description of Brahman can only be silence.

Despite the 'Not this, not this' nature of Brahman, the Hindu classics do contain various descriptions of him. Brahman is known as 'being', 'knowledge', 'bliss', 'truth', 'consciousness', etc. The Hindu-influenced Christian theologian R. Panikkar points out that without the knowledge of a personal God, Brahman easily becomes an empty abstract. It should be said however that Panikkar also remarks that faith in a personal God without the infinite indescribable Brahman can slip into a cheap anthropomorphic idolatry.

In non-dualistic Hinduism, Brahman is also known as Saccidananda, a word made up of the three parts *Sat, Cit* and *Ananda*. Saccidananda describes the one Brahman, but he/it consists of three parts. *Sat* means 'being' or 'truth', the force through which alone the universe comes into existence. *Cit* has the idea of intelligence and wisdom. It is the journeying aspect of Brahman. *Ananda* conveys a picture of colourful joy and beauty. The great Indian Christian theologian Brahmabandhab Upadhyaya (1861–1907) has sought to bend the three-in-one Saccidananda to fit the Christian Trinity. He uses *Sat*, the ultimate creative being and truth, to describe God himself. For Jesus Christ he sees *Cit* as the parallel, for it is the wisdom of God that journeys into the world. The colourful joy and beauty of *Ananda* brings the Holy Spirit to mind. Clearly there are some parallels between the Christian Trinity and Saccidananda, but we must not lose sight of the fact that Saccidananda can never be equated with the personal God of the Bible. Brahman differs considerably from the biblical God.

In passing it may be challenging to note that Western theological studies have still not discovered such great Indian theologians as Upadhyaya despite the fact that India was producing deep Christian thinkers and writers so long ago. The insularity of much Western theology is to be regretted. Yet today the Western world is strongly influenced by Asian religions and philosophies, so such Hindu/Buddhist-related theological thinkers should come centre-stage in our biblical and theological curricula.

b) Dualist Hinduism

A few years ago one of my students worked for a while in a very conservative evangelical Christian bookshop. In defence of theological purity they refused to stock books even by C. S. Lewis and others who might not be strictly evangelical. To the student's amusement however they did not hesitate to sell posters with verses from the Bhagavad Gita, a Hindu dualistic scripture. The Bhagavad Gita contains beautiful descriptions of a personal God whose concern for the world is evident. In dualistic Hinduism, Brahman's attributed form comes to earth in various incarnations of Vishnu in order to defeat the demons and save the cosmos. These incarnations take on a variety of forms – swan, fish, tortoise, man-lion and others. But the best known incarnation of Vishnu is the black and beautiful Krishna, whom the Gita describes as 'supreme and changeless'. We may well ask what is the relationship between Brahman and Vishnu. Vishnu the preserver joins with Siva the destroyer and the ultimate Brahman to form the threefold unity of Trimurti, the ruler of the universe with one body and three heads. Again we have something which approximates to the Christian Trinity, but which in fact differs considerably. And it has still to be said that the attributed and personalised form of Brahman remains a second best below the non-attributed *Na iti, na iti* Brahman. Hindu religious leaders therefore always feel that the Christian worship of a personal God never penetrates beyond the superficial to the mystical depths of the highest form of Brahman.

5. Buddhism

Out from the atheistic Samkhya school of Hinduism came the new religion of Buddhism. While non-dualistic Hinduism proclaims that nothing exists of itself except the ultimate Brahman, Buddhism goes one further. It denies that even Brahman exists. The ultimate reality is Sunyata, the absolute emptiness of the great void. Buddhism maintains that there is no first cause, no ultimate end – all is a wheel of becoming. There is no absolute, nothing ultimately is.

But it might be claimed that God by definition must be and not merely be 'becoming'. That which is only becoming cannot yet be absolutely perfect and therefore cannot be the ultimate God. It is therefore significant that in the Bible God reveals himself as the great 'I am', YHWH. And Jesus takes that title to himself in declaring 'I am the way, the truth and the life', 'I am the good shepherd', etc. The biblical God is not only becoming, he is. Otherwise he would not be absolute and perfect.

In Buddhism the apparent existence of the world and of ourselves is what binds us to the constant chain of karma, the law of cause and effect. All existence must then be considered undesirable. The Thai Christian theologian, Petchsongkram (in *Talk in the Shade of the Bo Tree*, Bangkok 1975) points out that to the Buddhist the act of creation must necessarily be something evil. The Buddhist may consider the creator of the world to be more devil than God.

But actually Buddhism denies that there ever was a beginning or that there will be an end. All is a wheel of becoming. A circle knows no starting point nor conclusion. In fact the Buddhist scriptures talk of a Brahma who thought he was the original creator, but actually he merely restarted the continual cycle of human existence.

We may notice that the Buddhist scriptures do talk of some sort of divine beings called Brahma. But these should not be equated with the biblical idea of God. They merely stand at a certain level on the ladder climbing towards enlightenment. Their particular rung may be higher than many of us have attained, but it remains lower than the attainment of Buddhist monks. So a Brahma may be reincarnated next time as a monk and only then is he likely to reach the enlightened state. Although this may be the common belief, Masefield (*Divine Revelation in Pali Buddhism*) shows that it is contrary to true Buddhism in which laymen, gods and even women may attain nirvana. But it is also true that even devas (gods) may have much dust in their eyes and thus be unable to receive the insights given by the Buddha and so be enlightened.

When one visits a Chinese Buddhist temple, it is quickly evident that worship and prayer is directed towards a variety of mythical gods in idol form. But in a Thai Buddhist temple one senses a totally different atmosphere, for this stream of Buddhism is more orthodox. Here the statue of the Buddha dominates. He receives the prayers and worship of the people. Is Buddha then equivalent to God? It is true that he is said to be *lokuttara*, or supramundane, and some feel that he never was fully human. In the Pali Canon Niddesa scriptures, the devas are discussed. Some beings are called 'deva' because this is the conventional title for all royalty. Others become devas by birth, including the Brahma-gods. Yet others become devas because of their purity in previous human incarnations. But above them all, according to the Niddesa, stands the Lord Buddha who is *the* deva, indeed the 'atideva', or super-god. And yet it seems self-evident from the Buddha's own teaching while still alive that he himself would never have accepted deification.

From the above it becomes apparent that Buddhism has little that can parallel the biblical concept of God. While the common charge that Buddhism is atheistic may not be altogether true, it is certainly clear that it contains nothing comparable to the biblical revelation of God.

Conclusion

We have looked briefly at various religions' answers to our original question, 'Who is God?' How then do we understand the clear teaching of the Bible that the Lord is king of all the earth? What is he like and is he the unique God? If so, are the gods of other religions mere idols?

The Bible makes it clear that there is one God who made the earth and all peoples. In the early chapters of Genesis he is acknowledged as the unique God of all. But then in Genesis 11 human pride in building the Tower of Babel led to God scattering the people and dividing them into different nations and peoples. But as we have already seen, belief in one Creator God remained deep in the consciousness of all peoples. This traditional memory became corrupted by sinful men and women and was often overlaid by the worship of all sorts of capricious spirits and lesser deities, but still the knowledge of God remained. In his grace, God also added to that memory by revealing something of himself in his Creation and in human nature, but again this too was corrupted by the warped eyes of sinful humanity. This means that as Christians we accept that the High Creator God of other faiths is indeed the one true God known to us in Jesus Christ and in the revealed word of the Bible.

The Gentile nations around Israel in the Old Testament tended towards the idea that each people had its own god. And each god ruled in its own particular territory. We see this delightfully illustrated in 1 Kings 20:23. The Syrians thought that the God of Israel ruled in the hills while their own gods had power in the plains. But the God of Israel gave his people victory both in the hills and in the plains, for he is God of all the earth. He reigns sovereignly over all peoples and looks for all to follow him.

The God revealed in Christ and the Bible is unique and universal. But what characteristics stand out as fundamental to his nature? Traditional Christian books about God detail the biblical attributes of God and we do not have space in this book to describe them. God is omnipotent, omnipresent, omniscient and all the other traditional descriptions of his being. We have also already noted the significant fact that God is personal and living in today's context of Eastern religious influences. He is also deeply involved emotionally in the affairs of his Creation, so he feels anger at human sin and rejoices in all goodness. He is neither impersonal nor coolly detached, because love lies at the very heart of his nature. Because of his warm love he delights to serve: the key title of the Son of God is 'the suffering servant'. And then we have already underlined the constant biblical emphasis on God's holiness and burning purity.

So we may outline a few fundamental characteristics of God revealed to us in his word. But God in his glory outshines anything we may say about him. Even biblical words only dimly reflect his splendour. Ultimately we can only truly see the fullness of the glory of God in the perfect person of his incarnate son, Jesus Christ.

4

Other Views of Salvation

In the last three chapters we discussed whether reconciliation to God can be found outside of Jesus Christ. We observed that this depends on whether we believe that people can discover God without Jesus Christ and the Bible, so we looked at other faiths' claims concerning revelation. The Christian would maintain that revelation should not only come from God, but should also have God as its object and so reveal the person of God himself. If revelation only reveals God's will (as in Islam) and not God himself, then God remains beyond human knowledge. So we came inevitably to God himself. In the last chapter we looked then at various faiths' understandings of the nature of God. Now we must return to the question of salvation. Having seen a little of what other religions have to say about revelation and God, it is appropriate that we ask what they understand by salvation.

1. Judaism

The great but controversial Maimonides taught that children may be encouraged to study the Torah by promising them a reward of nuts, figs or honey. So too we may be encouraged to follow God's Law in obedience by the incentive of reward in the world to come and by the threat of judgment for the disobedient. But Maimonides observes that we should really aim to serve God out of love, not because of fear of punishment or hope for reward.

Nevertheless the ancient sages and rabbis of Judaism have taught much about the righteous person's reward in the world to come and the threat of judgment in Gehenna. The *Encyclopedia of Torah Thoughts* talks of the world to come as the 'paradise of the hereafter', 'the absolute and incomparable beneficence that is immeasurable by any physical standard'. Maimonides too attempts to describe the glories of the promised Garden of Eden where spiritual delights are eternal and we shall know by experience the true being of God the Creator. In Berakhot 17a the Talmud envisages 'enjoying the radiance of the Divine Presence' in the supernatural fellowship of that world to come. Salvation is also seen as the final reuniting of the body to the soul, while the wicked will not be resurrected with the rejoining of their bodies to their souls. But despite this specific denial of the resurrection of the wicked, David Bleich in his *With Perfect Faith* shows that the wicked do suffer the eternal and everlasting punishment of fire in Gehenna.

There can be little doubt then that traditional Jewish thought foresees salvation and judgment relating to the after-life. But Ephraim Urbach in his *The Sages – Their Concepts and Beliefs* also points out that reward and punishment are both in the hereafter and in this world. In more recent Jewish teaching the emphasis has been placed more on this world. The promised Garden of Eden is seen as a renewed heaven and earth in which shalom reigns. This shalom consists of a new security, the righteous fulfilment of the Law and the removal of all idolatry. So the Jews look forward to the ideal day when Messiah will usher in the kingdom of heaven and inaugurate the reign of righteousness. In contrast with the Christian faith, Jews look rather for the shalom of the Messianic kingdom. Christians on the other hand emphasise salvation in and through the person of the Messianic King himself.

The Christian Church has tended to stress the role of the individual to the neglect of the group or community. So repentance, conversion and salvation all relate primarily to the individual believer. In Judaism however considerable weight is given to the community of the people of Israel. It is not only the individual Jew who follows or disobeys Torah. The people as a whole entity can follow God in righteousness or turn away from him in sin. The rabbis follow the Old Testament in affirming that God will show his mercy to Israel when she keeps his Law, but he will judge her when wickedness and idolatry prevail. The history of Israel demonstrates the truth of this. Again and again Israel turned away from God in rebellion and then duly received her just deserts in judgment. But when Israel repented and turned back to the Law of God, God delivered Israel from the hands of her enemies and blessed her land. The final work of God in salvation will not just be the raising of the dead from out of their graves to enjoy the eternal delights of the world to come – it will however include this salvation of individuals. But God's salvation will also mean the establishing of his kingdom on earth for his people Israel as a whole.

We have already suggested in passing that God's rewards and judgments are determined by the righteousness or wickedness of his people. The Talmud frequently states that 'Israel was worthy that a miracle be performed' (e.g. Berakhot 1:1) or that 'sin caused the miracle to be withheld'. In Sotah 1:7 the Mishnah typically teaches that, 'With what measure a man metes it shall be measured to him again.' The rabbis teach emphatically that God's judgments fit what Ephraim Urbach calls 'the principle of "measure for measure" '. And yet it needs also to be said that the rabbis struggled with the obvious reality that in this world the righteous often suffer more than the wicked. They therefore underline the truth that God may chastise those whom he loves in order to stimulate greater righteousness. So God's saving work in this world is not as clear-cut as might be expected.

Fundamentally however the principle remains: God saves the righteous in this world and in the world to come. But traditional teaching shows that he does not only save on the basis of good works. Salvation also stems from repentance and from suffering.

Repentance is one of the seven things said to have been created before the creation of the world. Repentance is preceded by the Law which requires and stimulates repentance which in its turn leads to the Garden of Eden in the world to come. Through repentance sins can be forgiven and so salvation can be granted.

Traditionally the sacrificial system has been replaced by the concept of suffering. Instead of the shed blood of the sacrifice atoning for Israel's sins, now her own sufferings can act as the prelude to God's blessing. Jesus himself saw the imprisonment of John the Baptist as the sign that the kingdom of heaven was at hand (Matt. 4:12, 17) and the New Testament shows how wars and tragedies will precede the final establishing of God's kingdom. Jews today may point to the agonies of the holocaust as the ashes out of which the phoenix state of Israel emerged. In this, Judaism and Christianity speak with one voice: only through suffering and death can we come into salvation and life. The radical difference lies however in the lack of an atoning sacrifice. For the Christian all salvation and new life stems from the redeeming death of Jesus Christ, the Lamb of God.

Like Judaism, Christians also believe that salvation applies not only to the after-life, but also to this world. We too affirm the present tense of John's Gospel, 'We have eternal life.' We would however reject a largely material understanding of salvation, for we too are deeply conscious that Christians may suffer every bit as much as non-Christians. In fact as Christians we are called to take up our cross in suffering and follow the crucified Jesus. As the Father sent him into the world as the suffering servant, so he sends us to suffer in service of God and the world. But our understanding of salvation is based on a new and eternal relationship with God through the forgiveness of our sin by the atoning work of Christ. This leads to a new life in his resurrection, a life in which we are being renewed into the very image and likeness of God (Col. 3:10).

We agree too with Judaism that salvation is not just for individuals. It means also a new righteousness in society both in terms of communal morality and also social justice. Righteousness and justice belong together. The Christian will however see this in universal terms rather than just being based on Israel. Indeed in every application of the idea of salvation the New Testament strongly maintains the universal nature of God's working. Gentiles can also be saved without joining themselves to the people of Israel. As Romans 11:30–32 declares, God's mercies reach out to Israel and to the Gentiles. God's salvation is international in scope.

2. Islam

If Judaism is primarily interested in salvation in this world and only secondarily in eternal salvation in the after-life, Islam reverses that. It too believes in a God who works mercifully for his people on earth and it looks for a future when idolatry will cease and Allah alone be praised. But eternal judgment is never far beneath the surface in a Muslim's consciousness. Paradise and hell remain firm tenets of faith.

In the past some Christians tended to portray heaven and hell in very materialistic terms, whereas today this is replaced by the more spiritual idea of perfect fellowship with God in praise, worship and holiness, or separation from him. Islam too has a long tradition of materialistic imagery concerning the delights of paradise and the tortures of hell. Some more Westernised Muslims today and some mystics are seeking to exchange these for a more spiritual imagery. The difficulty for Islam in this respect is that Allah is immeasurably great and high above his creation, utterly distinct from mere humans. Allah cannot even be reduced to the level of life in paradise, so it becomes hard for Islam to conceive of heaven as intimate fellowship with God. While mystic Sufis will deny this, it remains true for more orthodox Muslims.

Islam may take the issue of God's judgment and the after-life with great seriousness, but it is not as deeply concerned with the divine work of salvation. Little debate takes place in Islam as to how God may forgive us and bring us into eternal life. Perhaps the reason for this lies primarily in the Muslim view of the nature of humanity. Muslims exult in their positive understanding of human nature. Humankind possesses great dignity because we are made in God's form and because we are God's vice-regents on earth. Even angels fell down before Adam with reverence. While Islam recognises the weakness and fallibility of humankind, it nevertheless strongly denies the Christian doctrine of original sin. For example, in the 1979 Islamic Conference in Swanwick, G. Hekmatyar of Afghanistan read a paper in which he declared: 'No original, inherited sin stands between the individual and his destiny – for *nothing shall be attributed to man but what he himself has striven for* . . . Sin means no more than a lapse from the innate, positive qualities with which God has enhanced every human being.' (G. Hekmatyar's italics.) Those sins which result from human frailty need of course to be compensated for by our good works, but Islam sees no need for the atoning work of Christ to still the holy wrath of God.

In Islam salvation depends on two things. Firstly the Muslim emphasis on God's total sovereign power means that we rely entirely on his showing mercy towards us. But secondly, accord-ing to the hadith, the authoritative traditions of Mohammed's thoughts, words and deeds, 'Such as repent, believe and act aright, these shall enter paradise.' God generally shows his mercy in response to our good deeds.

It has been said that in Islam God's mercy is more that of a king exercising his prerogative of power than of a father who suffers with his children and loves them out of their disgrace. Sweetman in his *Islam and Christian Theology* maintains that in Islam 'there is no inward compulsion of grace within the being of God'. Like a Middle Eastern potentate upon his throne, God dispenses justice towards his people. In accordance with his own desire he shows mercy to some and judgment upon others. Nevertheless because he is generally a God of mercy he does more often show grace to those who submit to him and do good.

The mercy of God may be further stimulated by the intercessory prayers of his messenger Mohammed. Mohammed's prayers have power before God and therefore Muslims will often pray to Mohammed in order to ask him to intercede for them. Indeed Al-Ghazzali claimed that all Muslims will finally be saved because of Mohammed's intercessory prayers.

We have noted that salvation depends on repentance. If a person will turn from false religion and evil deeds to submit to Allah and his Prophet, then God may show mercy to him. But it should be noted that repentance must lead to the true practice of religion and to amendment of life. This means that death-bed repentance has no validity, for it leaves no time for the good deeds which must follow repentance. So Muslims find the New Testament story of the repentant thief on the cross quite unjust. He had no opportunity to do good deeds which might outweigh his previous sins in the divine scales of judgment. Muslims would therefore consider Jesus' words quite immoral, 'This day you will be with me in paradise.'

True repentance must lead to the first of the traditional five pillars of Islam, namely faith. Salvation depends upon a right belief in the creed of Islam which declares that there is no god but Allah and Mohammed is his apostle.

Then repentance and belief must result in submission to Allah and his commands. So the Qur'an assures us that the mercy of

God is 'nigh unto those who do well'. Sweetman says that in Islam mercy is the reward for good deeds. There is also however a more universalist tradition within Islam. This is represented by the famous commentator on the Qur'an, Al-Baidawi, who describes mercy as, 'That universal attribute . . . which the Almighty extends to all mankind, the wicked and the good, believers and unbelievers.'

But such universalist ideas remain outside the boundaries of mainstream Islamic thought. Generally, Muslims await the final judgment when their good deeds and sins will be weighed in the scales. Then too the angels will test their knowledge of the Muslim creed. And so God will consign some to hell and others to paradise.

As we have repeatedly noted, the Christian will see clear parallels between Muslim ideas of salvation and the teaching of the Bible. And yet even those parallels seem to diverge because of the different understandings of the nature of God and humankind.

3. Hinduism

As we have seen, Hinduism contains within its long history a rich variety of philosophical and religious streams, each of which will have a different understanding of salvation. Perhaps the key word in seeking to relate to this subject is *moksa*, which is often translated as 'release'. To many this word conveys a purely negative impression of freedom from the chains of karma, the law of cause and effect. In salvation from karma and its consequent chain of reincarnations one is released from self and personal identity in order to sink into the greater Self like a drop of water losing its separate being in the greater vastness of the ocean. The well-known writer on world religion, R. C. Zaehner, therefore says that salvation for the Hindu is, 'To achieve the highest bliss in which personality is lost in that which both underlies and transcends it.'

But there is also a positive aspect to *moksa*, which may take various forms in the different schools of Hinduism.

In the very early religious philosophy of the Rig Veda we find the god Indra elevated to the position of the one supreme God. It is he who defeats the great demon figure of Vrtra and thus saves the world and humankind from the clutches of demonic power. In this Indra stands above all other gods, for the lesser deities are defeated by Vrtra. Through Indra's conquest of the demons humanity is given a new freedom.

Klaus Klostermaier (*Mythologies and Philosophies of Salvation in the Theistic Traditions of India*) shows that the Vedas' concept of salvation is not restricted to freedom and blessing in this world, but also includes immortality in the after-life. He points out that, 'Many hymns in the Rig Veda speak of heaven and the beyond.' He shows from the Vedas that in the 'world of the fathers' the soul will again unite with a glorious body and enter 'a life of bliss, free from imperfections and bodily weaknesses'. The Vedic heaven is indeed a place 'where Brahma reigns supreme, where there is eternal light'.

In the later epic scriptures, salvation as the defeat of demonic powers is graphically depicted in vivid stories. Particularly the Goddess Devi saves the world and the whole cosmos from the demons through victories over them in battle. This theme is repeated in various of the myths concerning the incarnations of Vishnu on earth. So his incarnation as a dwarf tricks the demon to allow him control over the land he can step over in three steps. Then the dwarf shows his true nature as the god Vishnu incarnate, and strides out with three immense footsteps which encircle the whole globe. So he saves the universe from the demons.

In the higher non-dualistic stream of Hindu religious philosophy, *moksa* is no longer attained through the practice of traditional sacrifices nor by means of religious rites, but rather through the destruction of *avidya*, ignorance. When one relinquishes the ignorance which thinks that one has some separate existence and identity, then one can become aware that one is but a part of the great Self. So J. B. Carman (*The Theology of Ramanuja*) points out that identity with the supreme Brahman is the goal of those who seek salvation or *moksa*.

But how does one seek salvation? The Bhagavad Gita (section 13) lists some of the means towards enlightenment or *moksa*. In verse 24 it declares that 'by meditation some perceive the Self in the self' while 'others by the path of knowledge and still others by the path of works'. In the following verse the Gita shows that some people are ignorant of those more yogic paths to salvation, but 'they too cross beyond death by their devotion'. Here devotion is linked too to the practice of worship. The various streams of Hinduism have then developed different ways towards *moksa* – meditation, knowledge, works and devotion with worship.

a) Meditation

Traditional Hindu meditation aims to sink one's self-awareness in total absorption in that Brahman which alone truly is. So when one sees one's own self, it actually is not oneself but rather the great universal Self. So Hindu meditation does not focus positively on a scriptural word or an attribute of God as is often practised in Christian meditation, but rather seeks to go through one's inner self into self-extinction in Brahman. Then only Brahman exists. So salvation loses all personal identity and awareness in that absorption in Brahman.

How different from Christian concepts of salvation. The biblical revelations of the nature of God as 'I am', YHWH, leads on to the final destiny of humankind in being like the God who is. We are and shall be because ultimately God is. In salvation Christians lose their selfishness, but not their self.

b) Knowledge

In many ways it may be said that meditation depends on true understanding or knowledge. The non-dualist Hindu aims to understand the ultimate reality that all is Brahman. Our *atman* or self does not truly exist, but in reality is Brahman. When one becomes fully aware that nothing except Brahman is, then one relinquishes hold on separate existence not only of ourselves, but indeed of all things. In the realisation that all is Brahman one may experience release from the eternal chain of karmic reincarnation. The non-dualist Hindu may therefore consider the Christian promise of 'eternal life' as something of a threat. His view of *moksa* or release seeks an escape from being and reincarnation.

c) Works

Traditional Hinduism has developed the concept of *dharma*. This is often considered to mean the whole revealed way of life and religious practice. It is an all-embracing term. The exact definition of *dharma* can cause considerable disagreement, but the overall feeling of the word leaves little doubt. Does it include the caste system? Is *ahimsa* or non-violence the basic ingredient of *dharma*? What religious practices are included in it? Such questions elicit a wide variety of answers, but yet there remains an overall feeling that *dharma* consists of the variety of Hindu ways. Through observing *dharma* some may attain *moksa*.

Again we observe the difference from the Christian way where salvation comes entirely by the work of Jesus Christ on the cross and in the life-giving resurrection. This is then graciously applied to the believer by the loving mercy of God. The Christian gospel of salvation is centred on grace, not on works – although of course faith and salvation must be worked out in obedience and holiness.

d) Devotion

In the early Vedas much emphasis is placed on the practice of ritual sacrifices. So the Sama Veda and Yajur Veda outline the rituals of sacrifice, while the Atharva Veda gives versified spells for curing diseases and gaining other this-worldly benefits. These sacrifices were seen as repetitions of an original great sacrifice by which the universe came into being. So the sacrifices renew the creative process and give new life.

Later the ritual sacrifices were replaced by asceticism and other acts of devotion which demonstrated both self-sacrifice and worship. This was particularly directed towards the Avatara, the incarnations of Vishnu, of which Krishna is the best known. In these more dualistic streams of Hinduism it may be true that devotees have to merit their god's grace, but still *moksa* can be said to be a free gift in response to one's devotion and faith.

From a Christian point of view one notes that little is said about the problem of sin as a barrier between humankind and a holy God. Indeed, Hinduism lacks a belief in a truly righteous and holy God. Therefore its concept of salvation has little relationship to the biblical concept of personal morality or social righteousness and justice. A Christian view of sin is absent from Hinduism. As a result, atonement for sin through the sacrificial death of a holy saviour remains alien to Hindu thought

4. Buddhism

Hinduism divides into two major movements – the strict and orthodox non-dualists and perhaps in reaction to this the more popular dualistic devotion to personalised deities. So also Buddhism embraces two different forms. The stricter Theravada form of Buddhism rules in such countries as Thailand, Burma and Laos. The more popular and less orthodox Mahayana Buddhism merges in with other religions like the Chinese Taoism, the Japanese Shintoism and the Korean Shamanism in an often syncretistic fashion. Mahayana Buddhism has also split with many variations on its original themes. Thus Zen, Pure Land Buddhism and Tantric forms now not only influence the lands of Asia, but have also spread widely in the West. Closely related to Tantric Buddhism is the school of yoga.

In Buddhism it is customary to teach that enlightenment or

salvation comes through the so-called Four Noble Truths. The first truth is the universal nature of suffering. It is reported that the Buddha said, 'Birth is suffering, sickness is suffering, death is suffering.' In his basic book on Buddhism E. Conze states that, 'Suffering is the basic fact of life.'

The second truth is that suffering is caused by *tanha* – thirst or desire. Through desire we grasp after existence and all that goes with that existence. All feeling reflects our desire to be. Buddhists would have no hesitation in agreeing with psychologists that human beings have natural instincts which cling to life and crave food and sex as essential to life. But Buddhist teaching affirms that such emotions and desires produce the illusion of self-existence. And it is existence which inevitably includes suffering.

According to the third truth suffering ends when thirst ends. This may come about through the destruction of that ignorance which clings to the illusion that we exist. True knowledge means an awareness that ultimately nothing is. While non-dualistic Hinduism maintains that only Brahman is, Theravada Buddhism goes one step further. It describes the ultimate reality as *Sunyata*, 'the void'. Sunyata is closely related to nirvana, that Buddhist state in which there is neither being nor non-being.

Salvation from the suffering of existence is attained then by awareness of *Anatta*, 'Non-being'. This may be attained by following the eight-fold path which starts with right view and concludes with right meditation.

Peter Masefield argues that right view is the first step in the eight-fold path which leads to enlightenment because one is converted to the path of salvation through hearing the teaching of the Buddha and thus gaining a right view. This conversion will lead to full wisdom, right morals and true mental discipline. But salvation comes through the hearing of the Buddha's word which brings the hearer to an enlightened right view.

On the other hand Mahayana Buddhism would seem to have a greater emphasis on enlightenment through merit, particularly through religious activities and prayers. In practice we also find this true of most Theravada Buddhists in countries like Thailand. Sadly, theory and practice do not always go together in any religion!

In Tantrism much emphasis is placed on such religious ceremonies, prayers and trance-inducing activities as cause worshippers to lose self-consciousness and thus enter the state of non-being. The constant repetition of special spells of particular words or sentences can play a major role in self-emptying. The Lotus Sutra scripture is a well-known mantra of this sort and Chapter 21 of this scripture deals particularly with spells and mantras which can lead to a state of trance.

Zen Buddhism too seeks to lead its followers into the state of non-being through overcoming all self-awareness. So Christmas Humphreys, the leading British Buddhist, said that 'Zen is nonsense'. In Zen all the senses are overcome and thus one attains salvation from the suffering of being. Zen has particularly emphasised the need to desist from all struggling against anything. By passive acceptance of everything we can lose all emotion which ties us to existence. So the Zen saying states, 'Cranes have long legs, ducks have short legs.' We should not struggle against such apparent facts, nor should we desire any change or historical development. Acceptance can lead to the quietude of enlightenment.

Zen also teaches that means towards salvation may be used, but no means has in itself any validity. Thus meditation can prove helpful, but we are not enlightened by meditation. But meditation is nevertheless the basic Zen means towards that realisation of the Buddha-nature which lies in each of us. While it remains true that we do not exist, the Buddha-nature in us does.

Before leaving Buddhism we must come briefly to Amida Buddhism or, as it is often called, Pure Land Buddhism. This form of Buddhism is based on devotion to Amida, the so-called Buddha of the Eastern Region. Those who love and trust him will be led by him to the Pure Land after death. The Pure Land is a staging-post towards full salvation in nirvana. Devotion to Amida is shown by the constant repetition of his name day and night throughout our life in preparation for the moment of death when his name needs to lie on our lips.

Amida Buddhism stems from the Mahayana Sutra scripture in which one of the eighty-one Buddhas listed is called Lokesvararaja. He and one of his disciples designed a 'Buddha-field' more excellent than all previous ones. Lokesvararaja then became its Buddha and dwelt in this pure land of Sukhavati as the Buddha of infinite life and light. In a previous life he took forty-six vows to lead all who remember him to the paradise of Sukhavati in which they can be reborn.

Again we may observe that salvation comes through the grace of a Buddha, but related to the devotional works of his devotees. But again nothing is said about the sinfulness of human nature and the need for a saviour's atoning sacrifice.

Conclusion

Debate rages today among Christians on the nature of salvation. Does it simply mean that God gives eternal life to those who believe in Jesus Christ, his death and resurrection? Is it therefore a question of purely spiritual benefits resulting from the forgiveness of sins?

In his two books (the Gospel of Luke and Acts) Luke specially emphasises the fact of salvation through Jesus, so it is appropriate to take particular note of his writings. For Luke salvation is firmly based on relationship with God through Jesus Christ and it is evidenced by God's gracious work of liberating his people. Yes, he saves from sin, but he also saves from demonic oppression and from sickness and death. The key to Luke's view of salvation is in Luke 4:18–19 which seems to be the text on which Jesus' whole ministry is built.

In these verses we notice first of all that Jesus is the anointed one, the long awaited Messiah. He starts with the fact that 'the Spirit of the Lord is upon me'. His ministry of salvation comes from God by the Spirit and is the climactic fulfilment of all prophecy concerning the promise of the Messiah. So salvation cannot be separated from a God-centred spiritual approach. But it is not just individual spirituality in relationship with the heavenly Father. Salvation brings 'good news to the poor', 'recovering of sight to the blind' and liberty for 'those who are oppressed'. It comes to its climax in the introduction of 'the acceptable year of the Lord', the so-called Jubilee Year in which debts were forgiven, slaves released, family lands restored and thus grave inequalities and injustices put right. So salvation becomes a much fuller concept than just reconciliation with God, although it is certainly based on that. Indeed this manifesto for Jesus' ministry also stresses the need for a preached message of good news. The Messiah will 'preach good news' and twice it says that he will 'proclaim'. In Acts, Luke will go on to show that the preached message has as its foundation the need for repentance and faith in the atoning work of Jesus on the cross and in the Resurrection. But new life in and through Jesus Christ means not only personal salvation, but also social change for the poor, captives, blind and oppressed.

Then too the biblical revelation of the nature of heaven and eternal life stands out from other religious views on heaven. Other faiths have beautiful descriptions of paradise, but they are nothing compared to the glory of eternal worship with our heavenly Father and the Lamb in fellowship with all the saints and in absolute holiness. The Christian should be immensely grateful to God for the perfection of the Saviour himself, his saving work for us and the final glory of full salvation to which we look forward joyfully.

Throughout this book I have stressed that elements of truth and goodness remain in every religious faith, as indeed in all human beings. But I have equally underlined the all-corrupting nature of sin which perverts every truth. While for Christians the first two chapters of Genesis remain deeply significant in this matter, so does the third chapter. It is true that Chapter 3 means that all in the first two chapters is corrupted, but it is equally true that the first two chapters mitigate the fearful consequences of the third chapter!

We are not surprised then to note that the world's major religions contain many parallels to the Christian teaching on salvation. But we also observe that the Christian faith will radically disagree with each of them. No other religion has a saviour who can match the absolute sinless purity and holiness of Jesus Christ. No other religious saviour is both fully divine and fully human in every part. No other saviour has died in an atoning and redeeming sacrifice for the sin of all humankind. The Christian teaching on the saving death of Christ is unique.

5

The Old Testament and Other Faiths

For the Christian the Bible is the ultimate source book for the teaching of the faith. Facing questions about the relationship of Christianity to other religions, we are bound to begin by turning to the Bible. What does it have to say about the various religions practised by the different nations found in the Old Testament and by the Gentiles in the New Testament? Are they considered to be equally valid as parallel expressions of God's revealed truth? Should the people of Israel and the New Testament Church have truth to learn from these other faiths? Is the faith of Israel and the salvation of Jesus the Messiah for all peoples or is it just for the few? Should we expect people to be converted from other religions in order to find an absolute truth and salvation?

In this chapter we shall look at the Old Testament's approach to other faiths.

Genesis 1–11

Whether we consider the early chapters of Genesis to be historical or merely a form of pictorial teaching, we may agree that they form the biblical background to all peoples' history and religious development. While traditional understanding of Genesis 1–11 has stressed that the unity of all humankind has preceded ethnic diversity *chronologically*, it may also be said that these chapters demonstrate that humanity is to be seen *theologically* as essentially 'one' within our ethnic diversity. Be that as it may, the Bible insists that all nations stem from the fact of God's Creation and from the corruption of God's perfect purposes for the world through the sin of humankind. In the story of the Tower of Babel, God scatters the people. From then on human history evolves with a multiplicity of separate nations and peoples, each of which will develop its own language, culture and religious practice. We today are faced with the bewildering cultural and religious pluralism which raises deep questions, but we must not forget that behind the present pluralism lies the one common original history.

Knowing that all peoples have the same background in this early history, we are not surprised to find considerable parallels between religions. But we should note that these similarities are found particularly in the facts related to us in those early Genesis chapters. How then should Christians react to such apparent parallels between the Bible and other religious traditions?

Some more liberal Christians use this to demonstrate that the Bible is not unique. Indeed, they would claim, its writers came after some of the other Middle Eastern traditions and they borrowed from them. So the Bible does not contain divine revelation, but merely a Hebrew version of other older myths.★

Some conservative scholars will react against such denials of God's revelation in the Bible, affirming that there are fundamental differences between the biblical accounts and others.

★In common usage, the term 'myth' suggests a story without historical foundation or accuracy. In theological writing, however, it denotes any teaching of truths through stories or narrative-style writing (*cf*. Jewish Haggadic teaching in contrast to Halachah) whether this be historically accurate or not.

There can be no question then of the Bible having taken over other peoples' traditions. The biblical word, they affirm, is entirely God's original and unique revelation.

Might there be a middle way between these two extreme positions?

We cannot know exactly how Genesis came to be written, but it is possible that God inspired the writer to use other local peoples' myths as a basis for what God wanted to teach his people. Of course other nations' traditions contain assumptions which are alien to the faith of God's people. These would have been changed as the Spirit of God directed the writing of Genesis. Through the obviously changed contents of well-known stories the Lord would underline what he wanted his people to learn.

Whatever the historical facts that lie behind the stories of the early chapters of Genesis, we may ask whether there is some common historical background to all peoples. Is it possible that all have retained distant memories of early history, the Creation, the Fall and on to some scattering of the peoples as pictured in the story of Babel? Might this account for parallels between the various traditions passed on from generation to generation? But as these early stories passed orally from parents to children through the centuries, were the contents altered to fit the changing religious beliefs of the different races? However we interpret Genesis, those who believe in biblical revelation will maintain that God in his grace led the author to record exactly what God saw to be right and true. Whether this came about only through the God-guided memory of God's people through the ages, or whether the traditions of other peoples were also used, we do not know. We have no sure basis for determining then whether Genesis adopts and adapts other peoples' traditions or whether those other myths have corrupted the true story of humanity's common roots as found in Genesis 1–11.

Abraham himself originated from these surrounding nations who by then had strayed from the pure worship of the one

Creator God. As the Jewish Passover liturgy reminds us, 'Our fathers were idolaters.' Abraham's background must have influenced his understanding of God and the practice of his faith. So again we are not surprised if there are common elements between the Hebrew faith and that of surrounding peoples. It was from the children of Noah that the nations of the world emerged (Genesis 10). Traditional Jewish interpretation of this chapter has stressed that these descendants of Noah signify all the Gentile peoples. Later Christian thought has also noted the implication that the Gentile nations are included in God's purposes in history, for they share the same forefather. So Amos 9:7 notes that God was in the migration of the Philistines from Caphtor and the Syrians from Kir as well as Israel from Egypt. This verse has been used to deny that Israel's history is in any way unique as God's revelation, but the prophet is rather showing that due to her sin Israel has become just like other nations. He is not saying that God reveals and saves in other nations' history like he does in Israel's. The Old Testament consistently teaches that the Lord alone is God of all the earth and he has a unique covenant relationship with Israel.

Indeed, there are parallels between biblical teaching and the religions of other peoples. The whole idea of covenants is also found in other Middle Eastern religions. The biblical covenant has close parallels with local political suzerainty treaties. Martin Buber also points out parallels between God's kingship over Israel and the human kings of other nations. So Israel was led by a pillar of cloud by day and of fire by night. Then when Israel encamped, the presence of God settled right in the centre of the people. So it was with human kings at that time. They too marched in front of their people, but encamped in the middle of them. So Israel learned that God was her king. The Bible may use elements from the surrounding peoples, but it always gives Israel specific God-centred content.

But there are also elements of Israel's faith which are unique. So Genesis 1–11 underlines the absolute distinction between

God as Creator and humankind and the universe as his Creation. It shows the moral nature of God which forms the basis for the biblical emphasis that religion and ethics are inseparably bound together. God's holy character also leads to the realities of judgment as well as salvation. Genesis 1–11 lays the foundations for the unique teaching of the whole Old Testament. None of the other peoples held to a firm faith in one God alone. Other nations practised sacrifices, but Israel alone stressed the sacrificial system as an expiation for moral sin leading to personal reconciliation and a new relationship with God. The Hebrew experience of God's *chesed* (gracious, loving kindness) is also unique. This divine grace guaranteed not only God's acceptance of Israel, but also through the new covenant, promised in Jeremiah 31, guaranteed Israel's response to God with a new, cleansed heart. This in turn formed the background to the whole New Testament good news of the Holy Spirit's work in us. He makes us into new creations, enabling us increasingly to walk according to God's covenant. Other religions contain no equivalent to this central teaching of the Bible.

So we may say that the Bible contains much that is unique, but it also can take over some things from other backgrounds and give them new significance.

The Call of Abraham

After Babel, God narrows down his particular call through the choice of Abraham, the father of the people of Israel. God's promise to Abraham assures him that ' "by you all the families of the earth will be blessed" ' (Gen. 12:3). Controversy rages about this verse because the original Hebrew allows two possible translations – 'will be blessed' or 'will bless themselves'.

i) 'Will bless themselves'

On the basis of this translation some critics affirm that God's blessing would pass through Abraham and his children, but the nations would come into blessing by themselves without becoming proselytes or joining the religion of Israel. God's saving blessings, they suggest, would come to the various peoples through their own faiths without conversion to the God of Israel. The natural sequence to this understanding of Genesis 12:3 would be that today, too, people need not be converted to the faith of Jesus Christ, but could find salvation in their own non-Christian religions.

ii) 'Will be blessed'

This translation leads to the more traditional belief that the Gentile peoples were unable to 'bless themselves', but needed the saving work of God through coming into a living relationship with the covenant people of God. Faith in the God of Israel had to be linked with joining the people of God. This makes sense of Abraham's calling to be the father of many nations (Gen. 17:5; Rom. 4:17,18).

In Isaiah 19, God further promises to make himself known to the Egyptians and he calls Egypt 'my people'. But this knowledge of God is not in isolation from Israel and God's revelation to Israel. In knowing the Lord, Egypt was to worship with the Old Testament sacrifices, burnt offerings and vows. And they were to be joined to Israel (Isa. 19:24).

Likewise in Isaiah 53:11, the Servant makes 'many to be accounted righteous'. Some maintain that the vicarious atonement of the Servant allows the nations to be saved within their own religious traditions. But the chapter clearly teaches that the benefits of the Servant's sufferings come through the transgressors' relationship with the Servant – 'by his knowledge' may be translated 'by knowing him' (v. 11). Sinners need the Servant's atoning work and can only gain this through the personal relationship which comes with knowing him.

What then is God's purpose for Abraham and the people of Israel?* Although God's election was narrowed down to the covenant people of Israel, they had the responsibility to demonstrate to the world the glory of their God and thus draw the nations to join them in their worship of him. So the Law was given to Israel with the aim not only of pleasing the holy God by their righteous living as God's people, but the Law was, to be lived out 'in the sight of the peoples' (Deut. 4:5–8) so that the Gentiles might recognise that the Lord is the unique God. To be chosen meant to bear heavy responsibility, not just privilege. And the Old Testament unashamedly notes Israel's failure to obey God completely. Heathen practices were often adopted. So Amos declared in the name of God, ' "You only have I known of all the families of the earth; therefore I will punish you for all your iniquities" ' (Amos 3:2). Israel's communal life as a nation as well as the personal lives of each individual had to reflect the holiness and loving kindness of God. Worship of the Lord was to have a profound effect on every side of life – the social, political and economic as well as the religious. The nations' salvation did not come through their heathen worship, their religious sincerity or ethical high standards. It came when they were drawn to join themselves to Israel in faith, worship and holy obedience which would transform the whole of life. Israel's election had universal significance.

Negative Attitudes

Through the Old Testament there runs a clear thread which denounces the faiths of other peoples. In conquering the

---

* Johannes Blauw, in his *The Missionary Nature of the Church*, coined the terms 'centripetal' to describe God's calling to Israel, whereas the Church's outgoing mission to the world is described as 'centrifugal'. Following Blauw, the evangelical R. De Ridder, the Roman Catholics D. Senior and C. Stuhlmueller and others have made these expressions normative.

promised land of Canaan, Israel was warned not to accept the religious views and consequent moral degeneration of the nations they overthrew. God does not tolerate idolatry, human sacrifice, homosexual practice or other sexual perversions, fortune telling, divination or other spiritistic practices (Lev. 18:21–25; Deut. 12:29–31, 18:9–13). Because of their religion and its attendant moral degradation, God drove those nations out of Canaan and destroyed them in judgment. As Israel's history evolved, she slipped disastrously into the very danger of which she had been so carefully warned. The seductive worship of Baalim led the Israelites into fertility rites. They also easily fell into the accepted religious views of the surrounding nations who held that each race had its own gods and religion. If a nation prospered, all knew that its god had become more powerful than the others, so it was wise to incorporate that religion into your own. So syncretism flourished. And the history of Israel demonstrated that easy-going religious tolerance led to moral decline and consequently the judgment of God.

Urging Israel to trust, fear and praise the Lord alone, the Psalmist does not hesitate to mock the gods of other peoples in a manner which would be considered quite unacceptable in the modern day. In mission history however we read of many examples of missionaries who purposely showed the empty powerlessness of idols. The great Boniface dared to cut down the sacred oak. In North Sumatra the pioneer Neumann gathered the people and in the name of Christ strode across the sacred field, thus showing that the spirits could not harm the Christian. Today we talk of 'power encounter' as we confront and defeat the demonic forces of evil in the name of Jesus Christ. Psalm 115 contrasts Israel's God who 'does whatever he pleases' with idols which have mouths but cannot speak, ears but cannot hear, hands but cannot feel and which are just 'the work of men's hands'. Isaiah 44 likewise attacks the folly of those who use half a tree as fuel for a fire and the other half 'he makes a god, his idol' (NIV). Indeed, the Old Testament prophets continually warn of God's fearful judgment against the religiously idolatrous and morally evil nations around Israel.

Despite the warnings, Israel's tolerance of other religions continued. When they eventually returned from exile in Babylon therefore, it was determined that they should make a new start. This resolute attitude led them even to put away all the foreign wives they had married. They feared that like the earlier King Ahab they too might be seduced by the religious and moral practices of their wives' home backgrounds.

The Width of God's Kingdom

Despite this radically negative attitude concerning other religions, the Old Testament affirms that Yahweh (YHWH) is the universal God who reigns over all history and all peoples. He has power in the lives of individual Gentiles like Pharaoh and Nebuchadnezzar. He calls the heathen city of Nineveh to repentance and shows his grace to them when they respond with sackcloth and ashes. The prophets thunder out their message of divine judgment against the nations all around Israel.

Perhaps the most remarkable Old Testament word concerning God's relationship to Gentiles comes in Isaiah 45. Here the heathen King Cyrus is called 'the Messiah', God's anointed one. God takes him by the right hand and leads him into victory. But it needs to be noted that God's purpose here is, ' "that you may know that it is I, the Lord, the God of Israel, who call you by your name . . . I am the Lord, the God of Israel, who call you by your name . . . I am the Lord, and there is no other, besides me there is no God . . ." ' Though Cyrus does not know the Lord, God works for him with the aim that he may come to see that the Lord alone is God. And he is God's instrument to bring a new freedom and liberation not only to Israel, but also to the other captive peoples.

Frequently in Israel's history God uses other nations as his servants to bring judgment on the people of Israel. So in Isaiah

10 Assyria is called 'the rod of my anger'. Although the Assyrians do not at all recognise the fact, it is actually God who sends them against godless Israel. So also in Habakkuk 1:6 it is God who is 'rousing the Chaldeans' and who has 'ordained them as a judgment' and 'established them for chastisement' (v. 12).

Although Yahweh is fundamentally the God of Israel, his covenant people, yet he remains the Lord over all peoples everywhere. And he never loses sight of his saving purposes for all nations. In Old Testament times God's salvation comes in association with Israel through faith in Yahweh, the Lord.

The faith of the people of Israel does not come as something totally new to other nations. Somewhere beyond the pantheon of lesser idols and deities remains the Creator God known in Genesis 1–11. This High God may be concealed by the clutter of religious practices, but he is never totally lost. So it is that the Old Testament does not hesitate to take over the High God 'El' who was worshipped by Abraham and his idolatrous forefathers. In the early chapters of Genesis God is known as 'Elohim' while the name 'El' first appears in Genesis 14:18 when Melchizedek, King of Salem, appears on the biblical scene. It is this universal High God El who is later revealed to Israel as Yahweh (Ex. 6:3). Through his covenantal revelation as Yahweh, El becomes knowable and brings salvation to his people.

Just as the Canaanite and Phoenician High God El is accepted into the faith of Israel, so likewise in the New Testament the Greek 'Theos' is happily seen as the same as the Old Testament's Elohim or God. Of course corrupted understandings of his nature and ways of working needed to be corrected through the teaching of the biblical revelation. Both El and Theos are adopted and adapted by the people of God.

But how can people come to know El and Theos? The New Testament makes it clear that they can only be known through Jesus. If we see Jesus, we see God. He is actually 'Immanu-el', El with us. We might have expected Jesus to be called 'Immanu-Yahweh' – and he is the perfect 'I am' or Yahweh – but he is also the High God of all nations incarnate in human form to reveal and to save.

Actually the Old Testament also adopts two other names for God which were worshipped as the High Creator God of heathen peoples, namely Elah and Eloah. Thus Elah is first used in the Old Testament by Ezra and may have come into Jewish horizons during their exile in Babylon.

Interestingly the early missionaries of the tribes of Europe followed the biblical pattern of accepting the pagan High God, but making it clear that the understanding of his nature needed to be corrected in the light of biblical teaching. So today we all assume that 'God' or 'Dieu' or 'Gott' is the biblical Elohim. They were the names of the pagan High God of the European tribal religions before the coming of Christianity.

Perhaps we should note again at this stage that there is a limit to what can be adjusted to biblical faith from other religions. While the Creator High God is always accepted, the lower pantheon of lesser deities and idol figures is vehemently opposed. The Old Testament Baalim, Ashtoreth and Moloch must never cross the thresholds of biblical faith. In the New Testament the personalised Greek and Roman deities (Mercury, Jove, etc.) are anathema. So also in early mission to the pagan British, Thor and Wodun could be accepted into the days of the week, but were totally excluded from Christian worship.

Summary

In the Old Testament we observe both continuity from other faiths and a radical discontinuity which utterly rejects heathen idolatry and its consequent immorality and occult practices. Where the High God or other religious beliefs and practices are accepted, they always need some correction to compensate for the corruption of truth which inevitably accompanies human religion. In a later chapter we shall discuss the source of truth and beauty in other religions, but at this stage let us just note that in the Old Testament it is recognised that other religions can and do contain a belief in the Creator God as well as other elements of truth and godliness. But the Old Testament also remains firm in its assertion that human sin so distorts and distances God that he needs to be further revealed in his covenant with Israel and can only be truly discovered through association with Israel and its worship.

6

The New Testament and Other Faiths

Time marches on; and in the changing circumstances new temptations rear their heads to replace the former battles. The people of God can never relax their guard, settling back into an easy-going traditionalism. As we learn the secret of victory in one situation, new struggles come out to confront us.

So it was through biblical history. In the Old Testament, Israel succumbed to the temptation to compromise their unique revelation by adding the worship of other gods and idols alongside the Lord. This continued until Israel's exile to Babylon which cleansed away these idolatrous accretions. Then came a long period of history when the Jews were in danger of mixing Greek philosophies into the pure Hebrew faith. The early Christian Church inherited this temptation. By its use of the Greek language in the New Testament it inevitably had to relate its message to Greek thought forms. The early Christians faced the missionary issues of the relationship of the gospel to a new cultural and philosophical context. If they had preached in a totally Hebrew fashion without any adjustment to their Hellenistic context, they would have fallen into the trap of irrelevance. If on the other hand they overdid their emphasis on relevance without adequate biblical teaching, then they would compromise the faith. We today know the problem as we relate our expression of the Christian faith in the contemporary British cultural scene. So we are not surprised to observe that most of the epistles were written in order to counter heresy. And that heresy was not an outright denial of the biblical faith, rather it meant a mixture of revealed truth with pagan Greek thought.

The New Testament confronts two opposite dangers. At one end of the spectrum lies the temptation to syncretism, that compromised Irish stew in which revealed truth is thrown into the pot together with the Hellenistic religious worldview. At the other end of the spectrum lingered the snare of a narrow insularity. We have seen that in the Old Testament God longed for all nations to know his saving grace, but salvation was to be found in association with Israel, his covenant people. Jesus himself came not only as Israel's Messiah to bring salvation to his own people, but also to open the door of salvation to the Samaritans and even to the wider Gentile world. His teaching also relates to the current views of his age, but he in no way compromises God's truth – indeed, he claims to be the truth incarnate and so the unique way to the Father (John 14:6). Now in the New Testament some of the early Christians felt that the Church was just a Messianic Jewish sect. To be saved you needed to worship the God of Israel through faith in the Jewish Messiah and consequently obedience to the Jewish Law, including circumcision. By becoming a Jewish proselyte you could be accepted.

Much of the New Testament is written to attack such a blinkered vision. Modern critics wrestle with the question of universalism, debating whether God will save all people irrespective of their religion. But this was not a primary issue in New Testament times. The Early Church was much more concerned with universality, not universalism. Is the God of Israel also the God of all peoples? Is the Jewish Messiah also the Christ for all peoples? Can a Gentile become a follower of Jesus the Messiah without becoming a Jewish proselyte and being circumcised? Is it then right for Christians to preach the good news of salvation in Jesus Christ to all nations?

We immediately realise how pressing these questions must have been for the apostle Paul. Although he was thoroughly Jewish he was called by God to evangelise Gentiles. What would other people think of his work? Was he denying the Mosaic covenant, God's revealed word to Israel, if he did not teach Gentile converts to become proselytes and submit to circumcision and the Law?

1. Romans

In answer to these questions Paul wrote his letter to the Romans. He wanted to use the Church in Rome as a launching pad for further Gentile mission to Spain (15:24), so it was imperative that the Roman Christians should accept the rightness of his mission. Meanwhile he was about to take a financial gift from the new Gentile believers to the Jewish Church in Jerusalem (15:26–27), reminiscent perhaps of Isaiah 60:5: 'the abundance of the sea shall be turned to you, the wealth of the nations shall come to you'.

He starts his letter by affirming his divine calling to be an apostle, chosen by God to 'bring about the obedience of faith for the sake of his name among all the nations' (1:5). His purpose was to reap a harvest among the Gentiles (v. 13).

Romans 1:16–17 is often considered to be the text which the rest of the epistle expounds. These rich verses boldly assert that the good news of Jesus Christ is 'the power of God for salvation'. So Paul states confidently that he is 'not ashamed of the gospel'. In discussing the Christian attitude to other faiths this definite and positive view of the gospel needs to be underlined. But these two verses are not only giving us a firm affirmation of the gospel of salvation, but they also emphasise the universality of the message of Christ. Salvation comes to all who have faith, whether Jew or Gentile. 'To the Jew first and also to the Greek' is a major theme of this letter (e.g. Rom. 2:9–10; 3:9, 29; 9:24; 10:12).

Paul has stated that the aim of God's power in the gospel is 'for salvation'. From what do Jews and Greeks need to be saved? Chapters 1–3 give the answer. All peoples suffer from the same affliction. Sin is universal. Paul begins by showing the very worst of Gentile evil in the first chapter, but then proceeds to remind his readers that no one can say 'tut-tut' as they hear Paul's horrific catalogue of Gentile sins, both in false worship and moral iniquity. 'You have no excuse, O man, whoever you are, when you judge another' (2:1). In your own way you 'are doing the very same things'. The scandals of the cheap tabloid may titillate and give rise to a self-satisfied 'aren't people awful!' But Paul is underlining that all people of all nations share the same nature of sin.

The second half of Chapter 2 goes on to show that Jews are just as bad as Gentiles. This leads the apostle to his summary: 'all men, both Jews and Greeks, are under the power of sin' (3:9).

A universal problem merely leads to despair unless there is an answer which is available to all people. There is – and Paul now gives it.

Through Jesus Christ and his atoning death God gives believers his righteousness, his redemption. God provides through the blood of Christ a way of expiation and propitiation (3:21–26).

Paul goes on to show that this way of salvation is open to all people, Jews and Gentiles, because it comes through faith, not 'works of law'. If the Jewish Law, or Torah, formed the basis for justification, then it would just be for Jews and proselytes. And even for Jews possession of the law will not justify, for justification comes by such a faith as leads to obedience. But the way of faith is open to all peoples. Paul here not only emphasises 'works' but also 'law'. Traditional evangelical approaches have concentrated exclusively on 'works', stressing that we cannot earn our way to salvation by good works. This is of course true. But we must not ignore the other side of the coin. Because justification comes by faith and not by the Jewish Law, therefore the saving work of Christ applies universally to all nations and peoples. This fact is central to the New Testament gospel; it is the heart of the 'mystery of Christ' (cf. Eph. 3:4–6) that God desires to save people from all nations.

Paul proves his controversial point that justification is not based on Law, or Torah, by giving the example of Abraham. Abraham was justified by faith hundreds of years before God revealed Torah to Moses, so Abraham could not have been justified on the basis of Torah. It should just be noted that the justification of Abraham was not before there were good works, but before God revealed Torah to Moses – Adam and Eve, Cain and Abel or Noah could do good works, but they did not have Torah.

So we see that both Jews and Gentiles stand under the same judgment of sin. They also enjoy the same possibility of salvation by the one God (3:30) through faith in Jesus Christ and his atoning death. What then is the position of the Jew today? Are God's promises no longer valid for Israel? That is the question confronting Paul in Romans 9–11.

In these chapters Paul strongly opposes any suggestion that God has rejected Israel or cancelled out his covenantal promises to them. Having battled through other arguments he wins through to the great vision of God's purposes through history both for Jews and for Gentiles. Through the general rejection of Jesus by most Jews the door was opened for the Gentiles (11:11, 15), as he himself had seen at Antioch of Pisidia. He himself there had boldly declared to Jews who were opposing his message: 'we turn to the Gentiles' (Acts 13:46) and then quoted to them the prophecy in Isaiah, ' "I have set you to be a light to the Gentiles, that you may bring salvation to the uttermost parts of the earth." '

But Paul foresaw that his preaching to the Gentiles would provoke some Jews to jealousy and so bring them also to salvation (11:11–14). So salvation was to reach out to both Jews and Gentiles. The goal was that 'the fulness of the Gentiles come in. And so all Israel shall be saved' (11:25–26 AV). There seems to be a typical Hebrew-style parallelism between the 'fulness' of the Gentiles and 'all' Israel. The context of rejection of Jesus by the majority of Jews (e.g. Rom. 11:7–10) makes it impossible to interpret 'all Israel' to mean every Jew; but equally 'fulness' and 'all' can hardly signify just a tiny elect remnant. These verses have claimed a multitude of interpretations, but at least we may confidently affirm that they point to a future turning of multitudes of Jews and Gentiles to God's salvation. It has been pointed out that the name of Jesus Christ is not directly mentioned in Chapter 11. Some therefore suggest that Paul believed God would save at least the Jews without faith in Jesus Christ. The whole context however implies that 'salvation', 'the gospel' and cleansing from sin stem from God's grace through faith in the death of Jesus Christ.

Paul's climactic vision of God having mercy upon the multitudes of Jews and Gentiles fits in with other New Testament passages. We particularly note how in the Book of Revelation multitudes from all the tribes of Israel and from all nations will worship 'our God' and 'the Lamb' (Rev. 7:4–10). Just as the Bible starts with God's Creation which is the beginning of all peoples, so it ends with the heavenly vision of people from all nations worshipping God and his son Jesus Christ. God's universal purposes of salvation come through Jesus Christ.

Only through Jesus? (Rom. 1:20; 2:10–15)
While it may be agreed that God's saving purposes reach out to all nations, some Christians would query whether faith in Jesus Christ is necessary.

In these two much debated passages in Romans, Paul makes it clear that God's nature, power and deity are revealed through the created order. All people can see the wonders of nature and so also see something of God's power and character. Likewise in 2:15 it is clearly said that our consciences can tell us what is God's will according to his Law. And so it could be that Gentiles who do not have the Mosaic covenant will still fulfil the will of God. Their consciences tell them what the Law demands and they just do it.

Traditional theology has always maintained that God not only reveals through his word, but also through nature and through the human conscience. This is called either general or natural revelation. Something of the nature of God and his moral standards can be known in this way. But is this adequate? We looked more at this in Chapter 3, noting that both the natural order and our consciences have been corrupted by the Fall. In both therefore the revelation is mediated through imperfect channels.

The context of these passages would seem to demonstrate that actually sin prevails and general revelation does not lead to knowledge of God and his salvation. Chapter 1:20 is saying that people are 'without excuse' because they could have known something of God's nature through the created order. But actually, 'although they knew God they did not honour him as God . . .' General revelation merely makes human sin inexcusable. In Chapter 2 it is true that God gives 'glory and honour and peace for every one who does good' because he 'shows no partiality'. It is also true that Gentiles who do not have the Mosaic Law will be judged on the basis of the innate law in their hearts (2:14). But Paul at first assumes (2:15) that their conscience will then accuse them, although he then allows the possibility that it may 'perhaps excuse them'. Finally however it is the holy God himself who will judge. The tragic summary of these passages underlines the fact of universal and ubiquitous sin – 'all men, both Jews and Greeks, are under the power of sin . . . none is righteous, no, not one; no one understands, no one seeks for God. All have turned aside, together they have gone wrong; no one does good, not even one.' (3:9–12). If Paul's letter had stopped there, it would have been depressingly negative. Happily however he goes on to expound the glories of God's saving work in Jesus Christ.

2. The Gospels and Acts

Peppered with Old Testament quotations and references, Matthew's Gospel clearly aims at a Jewish audience. This view is underlined by the fact that the Gospel begins with a genealogy going back to Abraham, the father of Israel. This genealogy of Jesus ends with a very Jewish use of the number fourteen (Matt. 1:17) showing that Jesus is the doubly perfect Israelite or son of Abraham. He is also the doubly perfect Davidic king and saviour from God's judgment in the deportation to Babylon. He is the perfect climax and fulfilment of the calling of Israel. Then Joseph is told to call his baby 'Jesus' because he was to 'save his people from their sins'.

This very Jewish Gospel includes the teaching that Jesus was also to be the Saviour of the world, not just of Israel. Jesus' wider concern for the Gentiles relates intimately to his concern for the restoration of Israel. Already in the Old Testament and in Jewish rabbinic thought the Messianic kingdom was to bring salvation to Israel, but it also related to the Gentiles. The birds of all nations would find shade under the branches of the kingdom tree. So the crucified and risen Jesus will not only 'redeem Israel' (Luke 24:21), but also bring forgiveness of sins to all nations (Luke 24:47). In the Council of Jerusalem, James also quotes from Amos to show that the restoration of Israel involves the Gentiles also seeking the Lord and being called by his name (Acts 15:16–17). It is Matthew who quotes the prophecy that Jesus is called 'Emmanuel', the High Creator God of the surrounding peoples now revealed and present among us in the person of Jesus. He is not just for the Jews. In Chapter 2 Matthew tells the lengthy story of the Gentile Wise Men coming from the East to worship the baby Jesus. And at the start of Jesus' earthly ministry it is emphasised that the light has now come to 'Galilee of the Gentiles'.

Both in Matthew and Mark, Jesus finds loving friendship and comfort in Galilee, the area where most of his disciples came from. In Jerusalem he would have nowhere to lay his head, no home to rest in. The holy city became the place of persecution and death, while Galilee offered hope. No wonder Jesus told his disciples to go to Galilee to see him when he was raised from the tomb.

While Jesus felt at home in 'Galilee of the Gentiles', Matthew and Mark show him facing demonic opposition when he crosses the lake to the fully Gentile land of Gadara. Storms beat against his boat and in Gadara itself he encounters demons. Nevertheless Jesus does purposely enter Gentile territory to begin the kingdom's invasion of the Gentile domain.

As we read through Matthew's Gospel we are surprised how often Jesus refers to the Gentiles. So in Chapter 15 we have the remarkable story of Jesus healing the Canaanite woman's daughter and then feeding the crowd of four thousand in the Gentile area along the Sea of Galilee. In the concluding chapters of the Gospel come some remarkable words: 'this gospel of the kingdom will be preached throughout the whole world, as a testimony to all nations' (24:14); 'when the Son of Man comes . . . before him will be gathered all the nations' (25:31–32); 'wherever this gospel is preached in the whole world . . .' (26:13); 'Go therefore and make disciples of all nations' (28:19).

Luke has such an obviously Gentile axe to grind that many have assumed he must have been a Gentile himself. However, considerable doubts on this subject niggle the critics' minds and we must leave this question unresolved. But what is crystal clear is that Luke underlines the fact that Jesus saves not only the poor and women, but also Gentiles. The structure of his second book, the Acts of the Apostles, develops the theme that the kingdom reaches out from its Jewish base through the Samaritans and the God-fearing Gentile Ethiopian eunuch to the Gentile world. The power of the Holy Spirit at Pentecost is inseparably linked to the apostles being witnesses in Jerusalem, Judea, Samaria 'and to the end of the earth' (Acts 1:8).

The first three chapters of Luke's Gospel reflect a Jewish character, but the wider Gentile theme slips in: 'thy salvation which thou hast prepared in the presence of all peoples, a light for revelation to the Gentiles' (2:30–32); 'all flesh shall see the salvation of God' (3:6). In the Acts of the Apostles, Luke felt the need of a bridge between the description of the Church's mission to Jews in Chapters 1–7 and the outreach to Gentiles which begins with the conversion of Paul, the apostle to the Gentiles. So the mixed-race Samaritans and the God-fearing Ethiopian span the chasm between Jews and Gentiles. In his Gospel too, Luke feels the need to introduce the Gentile-related ministry of Jesus and uses the genealogy for this purpose. So Jesus' genealogy at the end of Chapter 3 goes right back to 'Adam, the son of God'. The father of all humankind is God's child. All nations should have God as their father.

Then in Chapter 4, Luke records the outset of Jesus' ministry. In his reading of the Scriptures in the synagogue at Nazareth Jesus stops before he reaches the verses in Isaiah which prophesy that the Gentiles will become Israel's servants. He then proceeds to remind the people how the Prophet Elijah was sent to a Gentile widow rather than to a Jewish home, and Elisha healed the Syrian Naaman rather than any Jewish leper. So Luke underlines the fact that Jesus' ministry will save not only Jews, but also Gentiles. We see this also in Luke 9 and 10. Jesus sends out the Twelve (9:1) to preach the kingdom and to heal. In Luke 10:1 he then sends out seventy or seventy-two others also. Whereas twelve is the symbolic number of Israel, the rabbis considered seventy or seventy-two as the number of the Gentile nations – interestingly, too, the first translation of the Hebrew scriptures into a Gentile language, the Septuagint (the Greek Old Testament), was translated by a body of seventy or seventy-two elders. Again Luke carefully places a Samaritan incident (9:51–56) between the Jewish twelve and the Gentile seventy. So Luke stresses the universality of Jesus' ministry.

Is the 'Unknown God' Enough?

a) Acts 14:15–17
It has been noted that Barnabas and Paul seem to have made no attempt to preach Jesus Christ to the Gentile crowd in Lystra. It is indeed true that these verses record only the apostles' call to stop offering sacrifices to them as if they were the gods Zeus and Hermes. The content of the apostolic message here was twofold: 'Turn from these vain things' and 'turn to a living God', the Creator of all things.

While it is true that in this first recorded message to Gentiles there is no mention of Jesus Christ at all, two things need to be said. Firstly this short sermon emerged in a situation of urgency. The people of Lystra wanted to offer sacrifices to the apostles, thinking they were gods. At first Paul and Barnabas do not seem to have realised what was happening. Then they reacted with an unprepared call to the people to desist – this was no careful well-structured gospel presentation! Then too we note that they had previously 'preached the gospel' (14:7), so evidently they saw the need for Gentiles also to hear the good news of salvation through Jesus Christ.

b) Acts 17:22–31
In these verses we are given the second recorded message to a Gentile audience. It has been claimed that again we have no direct mention of Jesus Christ and also that Paul seems to accept the truth and reality of the Athenians' religion.

i)   While it is true that Jesus is not mentioned by name in this sermon, he is clearly presented as the final judge of all. The climax of the message is the resurrection of Jesus from the dead. It was this presentation of the Resurrection which divided the audience; some mocked while others wanted to hear more and eventually came to faith (17:32–34). This emphasis on the Resurrection fits Paul's previous preaching in Athens (17:16–18). He so stressed Jesus and his resurrection that the Athenians thought he was bringing them two new gods, 'Jesus' and 'the resurrection'. Clearly therefore Jesus Christ was central to Paul's message to these Gentiles in Athens.

ii) Paul evidently did use the Athenians' belief in the unknown god as a bridge to the proclamation of the biblical God of Creation and then also to the resurrection of Jesus. We have already observed how the Old Testament took over 'El' and filled this High Creator God with the full biblical revelation of God's nature and character. Now Paul has no hesitation in linking the Athenians' unknown god to their belief in a 'God who made the world'. He then teaches them more about the God of Creation and leads them on to faith in Jesus Christ.

Having been a missionary among tribal people myself, I see exact parallels with much of the Church's evangelistic preaching in the area of Indonesia where I worked. People there too believed in 'Dibata' who made the world. Christians then taught about his character as revealed in the Bible and supremely in the person of Jesus Christ. There is always some continuity between other faiths and Christianity. But still people need to repent and believe in Jesus Christ as Lord and Saviour.

3. John's Gospel

It is often claimed that John's prologue (1:1–18) forms the text which is then expounded in the rest of the Gospel. It is good therefore that we look more closely at these verses.

John starts with a clear reminder of the Creation in Genesis: 'In the beginning . . .' When Luke records Peter's account of the conversion of Cornelius, that early Gentile convert, he too uses these words 'in the beginning' (Acts 11:15). So John begins with the creation of the whole world and all peoples. From this foundation he builds the theme of the universality of God's purposes in Christ. Jesus is not just the Saviour of the Jews.

John goes on to underline the universal significance of that creative Word which became incarnate in the person of Jesus Christ. The repeated 'all' disallows any narrow insularity – '*all* things were made through him' (1:3); 'that *all* might believe' (v. 7); 'the true light that enlightens *every* man' (v. 9); 'to *all* who received him' (v. 12); 'from his fulness have we *all* received' (v. 16). This emphasis is reinforced by the fourfold 'world' in verses 9–10. And he omits the word 'earth' or 'Erets' which is stressed through frequent repetition in Genesis 1 and 2 (used twenty times in Genesis 1 and a further six times in Genesis 2). This word had become so closely connected with Israel in the term 'Erets Israel' that its use in John 1 might detract from John's whole purpose.

The light of life shines so gloriously that even the darkness cannot overcome it (1:5). Clearly John is referring here not only to Genesis 1, but also to Isaiah 9 in which the light of God's active presence brings salvation to his people through a son whose name will be 'Wonderful Counsellor, Mighty God, Everlasting Father, Prince of Peace'. He will sit on the throne of David and establish a kingdom of justice and righteousness. Our hearts throb with excitement when we learn that this true light was coming not only to Israel, but also into the world. Our joy gives way to the anticlimax of tragic pathos. The true light had created the world and yet 'the world knew him not' (v. 10). He came to his own people and incredibly they 'received him not' (v. 11). Despite the long centuries of God's preparation for the coming of the Messiah, Israel still rejected him.

But now John goes on to declare that the door is open for Gentiles who are not blood-born children of Abraham, but they too can become God's children by receiving Jesus Christ and believing in his name (1:12). In the Old Testament Israel had been called to be God's children, but now Gentiles too can enjoy that immeasurable privilege. The world which 'knew him not' and Israel who 'received him not' can now gain both grace and truth through Jesus Christ (v. 17). They can now know God the Father because Jesus Christ has 'made him known' (v. 18).

So the prologue to the Gospel stresses Christ's universal mission. The first twelve chapters conclude on the same note. Only then does John move on to the climactic final act, the death and resurrection of Jesus.

In John 12:20 some Greeks came to Philip asking to see Jesus. Evidently Philip hesitated because he knew that Jesus had not easily welcomed the Canaanite woman in Matthew 15. Would Jesus now refuse to see these Gentile Greeks? He had said that he was sent only to the lost sheep of the house of Israel (Matt. 15:24). So Philip shared his predicament with his brother Andrew and they went together to Jesus. How did Jesus respond? ' "The hour has come for the Son of man to be glorified" ' (John 12:23).

Jesus' reaction seems at first sight to be somewhat over the top. After all, it was only a few Gentiles coming to see him. Why then was he so excited?

Jesus knew the Old Testament dream that the Gentiles would be attracted to the glory of the God of Israel in Zion. The light shining in the life of God's people would draw the Gentiles in like bees to honey. Now these representative Gentiles were coming in not just to Zion, but to the Lord of Zion. The Old Testament was being fulfilled, so now the way was open to introduce the new covenant in the shed blood of Christ.

In John 12, Jesus goes on to point out that his sacrificial death would 'bear much fruit' (v. 24) and would bring eternal life to 'any one' who follows him in sacrificial service (v. 25–26). In his crucifixion he would draw 'all men' to himself.

So John's Gospel underlines this truth – the saving death of

Jesus Christ has universal validity. This is the way of salvation for men and women of every background everywhere.

Universal Light?

'The true light that enlightens every man was coming into the world' (John 1:9). It is rightly pointed out that in John's prologue the Word and the life-giving light antedate the incarnation of Jesus. Some draw the conclusion that throughout history there is a non-incarnate cosmic Christ which enlightens people not only of all races, but also of all religions. But John is not talking about enlightenment through other *religions*. He is saying that God's light shines to all *people*. In a later chapter we shall look further at this theological viewpoint, but meanwhile we need to make three points:

i) It is true that God is sovereignly active beyond the narrow borders of the synagogue and the Church. God works in grace among all people. His light shines everywhere, sometimes more brightly and sometimes in a more muted fashion. This does not necessarily mean however that other religions equally offer a revelation of God which suffices as God's way of salvation. Indeed, as we have seen, human religion may actually dim the light of God and stop people seeing his salvation.

ii) We must not take John 1:9 out of its context. We cannot separate the creative word and the light of God from the incarnate Son of God, Jesus Christ, who is the Word made flesh. Our theology cannot ignore the historical facts of the birth, life, death and resurrection of Jesus. It was when he 'came into the world' that people could receive him by faith and thus become children of God. In fact the prologue ends with the statement that 'no one has ever seen God', but the Son of God has made him known (John 1:18). For this reason the word became flesh, that we might be enabled to see the glory of God and receive the fullness of God's grace (John 1:16). Such glory only becomes possible through Jesus Christ and what he has so wonderfully done for us.

iii) In early Jewish thought it was sometimes considered that Moses was the light of God because God used him to bring the Law to Israel. Now in John 1:9 we are shown 'the true light', Jesus Christ, who is not only the second Adam and perfect man, but also the second Moses, the true light. Jesus brings the perfect revelation of God to enlighten and save beyond the borders of the people of Israel. In Jesus Christ the light was coming into the world for all people, Jew and Gentile alike.

Exclusive Verses

The liberal Catholic writer Paul Knitter in his very helpful book, *No Other Name*? says, 'Much of what the New Testament says about Jesus is also *exclusive* . . . Jesus is the "one mediator" between God and humanity (1 Tim. 2:5). There is "no other name" by which persons can be saved (Acts 4:12). Jesus is the "only begotten Son of God" (John 1:14). No one comes to the Father except through him (John 14:6).' He goes on to declare the New Testament emphasis that as all died in the one man Adam, so all will be given life in the one man Christ (1 Cor. 15:21–22), for the work of Christ was 'once for all' (Heb. 9:12). Jesus is the 'final word for all who preceded or may follow. To close one's eyes to such proclamation is either psychologically to repress or dishonestly to deny what one does not wish to face.'

Having made this strong statement, Knitter then argues that actually these verses have no validity for today. He feels that such exclusivist statements were the natural way of talking for the early Christians, as indeed in what he calls 'classicist culture' throughout history until the modern age. But in our day we do not use language in such ways and therefore we can reinterpret these verses. He claims that texts teaching the uniqueness of Jesus as Lord and Saviour merely reflect the language of the day, but do not literally mean what they seem to say. So he states that they 'pertain more to the *medium* used by the New Testament than to its core *message*'. So Knitter feels that these verses demonstrate the early Christians' commitment to Jesus Christ rather than to any belief that he is the only and unique Lord.

But we have to ask whether Knitter is being honest with the text. Is he biased because of a particular axe he wants to grind? As we go through his book we find his ulterior motive coming through loud and clear. His aim stands out that 'doors would be opened more widely to dialogue with other believers equally committed to their saviours'. And his view of dialogue precludes the possibility of a convinced faith in any absolute or in a unique saviour.

We come back therefore to Knitter's affirmation that we have to take seriously the New Testament claim that Jesus Christ is indeed the one mediator between God and humanity. He is God's only Son, the unique sacrifice for sin, the one way to the Father. The New Testament does not allow us to place Jesus on a level with other gods or saviours.

In Ephesians 3:19, Paul longs that the Christians may share with all other Christians the knowledge of Christ's love and thus 'be filled with all the fulness of God'. Strangely, Knitter manages to assume that this verse means that it is non-Christians who will have this experience of God's fullness. But Paul is clear. As we have God's Spirit in the inner person and Christ dwelling in our hearts through faith, then we shall know the love of Christ and be filled with all God's fullness. Through this Trinitarian experience of Father, Son and Spirit we may have the fullness of God. There is no other way to know God in his fullness.

The message of the Bible is indeed an exclusive one. We see this not only in the verses rightly quoted by Knitter, but also in the fundamental teaching of the whole Bible. The Old Testament stresses the unique claim of the God of Israel to be the only true God. And Israel is his one covenant people. Jesus is shown in the New Testament to be the only begotten Son of God, the unique incarnation and full revelation of the one God. He is also the one seed of Abraham, the perfect Israelite – the unique fulfilment of the one covenant people of God.

Conclusion

In these last two chapters we have seen how the Bible starts with the Creation of the world and of Adam, the father of all humankind. Only with the particular call of Abraham does the story narrow its universal scope. Then God's call to Israel does not allow any proud or insular exclusivism, for God aims to demonstrate his glory to all nations through the life of his elect people. He wants to draw all peoples to himself. Then in the New Testament we see God's purposes pushing outwards in ever-widening circles. The Jewish hub radiates out through the half-breed Jew-Gentile Samaritans to the wider Gentile world. God's revelation in Jesus Christ brings salvation to Jew and Gentile alike. Jesus had foretold that in being raised up on the cross he would 'draw all men' to himself (John 12:32). So the Early Church took the good news of salvation by Jesus' death and resurrection out to the world. While the apostle Peter concentrated on preaching to Jewish communities, Paul went to the Gentiles. Tradition tells us that Mark took the gospel down into Egypt, while Thomas followed the trade winds across the Indian Ocean to plant the Church in south India. The first Christian kingdom was established in Edessa, north-east of Israel.

The apostles and Early Church understood the clear message of the Bible. They knew that the life-giving message of salvation in Jesus Christ had to be preached to all peoples everywhere, Jew and Gentile alike.

7

Other Faiths: Demonic, or Another Way to God?

As one who teaches other faiths in a mission training college, I am impressed by my students' reactions. Often they comment that such studies have made their own Christian faith come alive in new ways. Contrast and comparison with others gives us a greater understanding of ourselves. As Knitter points out, 'To answer the perennial question "Who am I?", we have to ask the question "Who are you?" '

In examining particular aspects of the various faiths, we have to ask ourselves first what our attitude should be to these religions. Knitter suggests that there are three popular attitudes towards other faiths.

a) All religions are relative
Knitter cites Ernst Troeltsch (1865–1923) as his case study for this approach to the religions. Although Troeltsch represents a bygone stage of philosophical and theological development, his views still live on today.

Like many contemporary thinkers in our time, Troeltsch disliked the idea of a powerful, sovereign God standing above and outside history who could then intervene in human affairs. He rejected any thought of what Knitter calls a 'God swooping down from heaven and intervening into history at particular spots'. He would rather feel that people's religious sense expressed in their different faiths is actually God's universal revelation at work within all humankind. So there is no absolute revelation or truth. Nevertheless there may indeed be a final absolute goal which remains beyond our knowledge and lies outside this world. Meanwhile all religions contain aspects of truth, while no religion has the truth.

Troeltsch realised however that this denial of any absolute truth known to humankind causes problems. How can we determine truth from error or good from evil? If the religions disagree, how can we determine which is right? This led him to confess at first that Christianity is the highest of the religions and superior to other faiths. So other beliefs could be put against the standard of Christian ideas. Later however he retracted this. Troeltsch assumed that Christianity and Western culture are somehow one indivisible entity, so to assume Christian superiority means a racialist pride in Western culture. Many today would hold this position.

b) All religions are essentially the same

Knitter picks the historian Arnold Toynbee (1889–1975) to represent this second, still popular view. Toynbee rightly notes that within all humankind lies a deep religious nature. This universal spiritual presence, he maintained, not only contained 'non-essential practices and propositions', but also some 'essential counsels and truths'. These fundamentals are common to all religions. He particularly saw four common factors:

i)   Religion stems from the incomprehensible mystery of the universe.

ii) The meaning of the universe may be found in some Absolute

Reality which relates to the world, but which remains separate from the world.

iii) This Absolute Reality contains the truth and goodness for which all humankind yearns. All religions provide a way to bring humankind into harmony of relationship with this Absolute Reality.

iv) The way to such harmony lies in the denial of self-centredness, finding a new central point for life in the Absolute Reality.

Of course Toynbee saw considerable discrepancies between the different religions, but he considered these to be non-essentials. As we all become aware of the non-essential nature of these differences, we may learn to concentrate on the core essentials which unite us. Then we will be able to make a common stand against our new adversary, the 'revival of the worship of collective human power, armed with new weapons, both material and spiritual'. In this struggle there can be no sense of one religion being in any way superior to any other, for all are essentially the same.

Comparative religious teaching today often shares this view. It seeks to show that despite some relatively minor differences all religions share the same basic truths. As we have seen in Chapters 2–4, such a view is shallow and ill-informed, not doing justice to any of the religions it deals with. We need to approach the beliefs and practices of the various faiths honestly, not watering them down to fit some mythical common denominator.

c) All religions share a common psychological origin

Here Knitter takes Jung as his example. Jung taught that our ego is the image of God and thus also the revelation of God within the human unconscious. This inevitably implies a denial of any objective revelation from outside. Because all humankind equally has this religious nature within our unconscious all religious awareness carries equal weight and validity. All religions therefore contain truth and one is as good as another, for they all stem from the same psychological origin within us.

Jung's belief in the equality of all religions leads inevitably to a strong denial of Jesus of Nazareth as the only Christ symbol. The universal Christ may be incarnate and revealed to different people through a whole variety of religious figures – Jesus, Mohammed, Buddha or Krishna. Jung particularly advocates Christians learning from Zen Buddhism with its ability to relate to the human unconscious.

We need hardly state that Jung's approach to other religions throws the unique redemptive work of Jesus Christ out of the window. He would definitely deny the objective fact of Christ's death on the cross as God's sacrifice for the sin of all who will believe in Jesus Christ as Saviour.

Knitter is right in saying that these three views are common today in our society. Christians certainly need to apply biblical teaching to such ideas. But this means that we have to be clear in our own minds how we view other faiths.

It seems to me that three possible approaches present themselves. All are commonly met in our churches.

1. They Are Demonic

The stern face of an ayatollah frowns at us threateningly from our TV screen. In front of him huge crowds of Iranian Muslims shout their fanatical approval and their unswerving faith in Allah. The cry 'Allahu akbar', 'God is the greatest', sends nervous shivers down our rather weaker spines. In such contexts it is not easy for Christians to appreciate that to some extent we agree with those crowds. We share the belief that God is indeed the greatest, although our understanding of this expression will differ considerably from theirs. When faced with this aggressive call to unswerving allegiance to the God who is incomparably great, we are unlikely to shout 'Amen'. The shiver down our spines moves us rather to counter-attack with the accusation, 'It's demonic.'

Some Christian books use the figure of an ayatollah on their covers to warn Christians that Islam threatens our whole way of life and our Christian faith. Peaceful co-existence with Islam, they point out, is like going to bed with a tiger. The crusading mentality is easily aroused as they call us to spiritual battle against Satan and his Muslim forces. As Christians constitute the army of God, Islam is a Satanic enemy power. The horror of suicide bombings in New York, Washington and elsewhere have heightened Christians' sense of the evil within Islam. This is further exacerbated by the knowledge that our Christian sisters and brothers in Muslim countries frequently face horrendous discrimination and persecution.

This impression is heightened by reports of Islamic law in practice. The film *Death of a Princess* correctly portrayed the reality of a Saudi Arabian princess who was executed publicly for adultery. Likewise public floggings horrify us all. In Sudan in the mid-1980s the government brought in full Islamic law, importing a special machine from Saudi Arabia for the cutting off of hands. Great crowds would gather to applaud when a criminal's hand was cut off and raised on high before the people. These baying Muslim crowds differed little from the Roman mobs calling for Christian blood in the arena – or Christian crowds calling for Jewish blood or enjoying the public execution of criminals in earlier centuries. Such fearful scenes may convince the Christian today that surely Islam is the tool of Satan, but we have also to say that all mobs easily demonstrate demonic outworkings.

In a large London shop a little cluster of Muslim women attracted our fascinated attention. Their shapeless black attire was topped by black headcoverings and black veils over the faces. We felt that a foreign and alien force was invading our land. With cool confidence they were challenging our whole value system, its belief in freedom and its struggle for the equality of women. We sensed a proudly aggressive threat against our culture and our faith. We knew too that Islam does indeed challenge the Christian Church in Europe, having declared the West as the primary object for Islamic mission. When Christians are threatened and afraid, it is easy for them to pronounce the other faith to be demonic.

A few years ago I had to drive through the château district of the Loire in France. I stopped to admire various of the castles I had visited as a child many years ago. While it was nice to see the pretty ones, I always love those castles which have huge thick walls atop mighty rock cliffs. Their fortress towers stand with such mighty pride and impress us with their power. As I stood in the sunshine below one such rugged fortress, a new thought came to me. As a peaceful traveller it was beautiful, but what would I have felt if I had been a soldier trying to attack it? I pictured an ancient army with bows and arrows facing those rugged walls. The officers said the bows and arrows were an all-conquering weapon in our hands, but the fortress seemed to laugh at their words. How the soldiers hated those fearful impregnable walls that made them feel so puny.

Do Christians feel like that with Islam? We are told that our God has given us all-powerful weapons with which to pull down all fortresses, but somehow Islam seems to stand against us unmoved. In many countries it is more likely that Christians will convert to Islam than Muslims to Christ. Islam defies the Christian faith, firmly denying the fundamental biblical doctrines of the Trinity, the deity of Christ, the atoning death of Jesus and original sin.

Facing the fortress of Islam the Christian cannot view it as a casual tourist, admiring its proud strength in the warm sunshine of uncaring indifference. We grieve that Satan uses this religion to keep millions of men and women away from the life-giving salvation of Jesus Christ. It hurts us that our Lord Jesus is made to look so puny and his glory pushed into the mud. And we know that indeed many Muslims are caught up in the demonic activities of popular Folk Islam.

So it is easy to dismiss Islam as demonic.

In a different way Eastern religions too may be considered

demonic by Christians. We may be repulsed by the sight of Theravada Buddhists offering joss-sticks before huge Buddha statues. To our eyes the multitude of idols reverenced in Mahayana Buddhism and Hinduism appear grotesque and it is easy to discern demonic powers lying behind such worship.

While some in the West are deeply attracted to the quietistic peace and spirituality of Eastern religion, others find the philosophical beliefs almost incomprehensible. The whole basis of Eastern philosophies differs from the Greek, Latin and Hebrew foundations of Christianity. So there is a tension. In one way we are attracted by the meditational devotion and the non-worldly peace, but at the same time the alien nature of Eastern beliefs baffles us. Many see in this the work of Satan whose deceptions are often cloaked by his character as the angel of light.

In Western countries Eastern religions have often gone hand in hand with the counter-culture of disillusioned middle-class youth. Their escape into the unreal dreams of Hindu sects or Buddhist yoga and meditation has often been closely tied to occult spiritism and the use of hallucinatory drugs.

In Hinduism and Buddhism, as also in Islam, spiritistic and magical practices abound. When one witnesses a Hindu walking barefoot through a pit of red-hot coals without harm, the reality of spirit power cannot but impress. The sight of a Buddhist in trance levitating in the temple sends shivers down a Christian spine. In Islam too the spirit world is invoked through the symbol of the hand of Fatima and the magic use of Qur'anic verses.

Satan may also be at work in other faiths in less obvious ways. He may lead people into the blind alley of a religious or philosophical system in which God is not truly known, salvation not obtained and social well-being not improved. Such systems may prevent people from coming into the life-giving faith of Jesus Christ.

It is not surprising then that many evangelical Christians dismiss these other faiths as utterly demonic and want to have nothing to do with them.

But we have to ask: is this approach truly biblical? Should we allow it to deter us from serious study of other faiths? And should we not still work for loving relationships with their followers?

2. They Are of God

While conservative evangelicals may tend to attack other religions as demonic, more liberal Christians bend over backwards to show tolerance. Some will try to show that actually all religions are similar and they will water down the apparent contradictions between the faiths. Others will agree that there are enormous differences and disagreements between the various beliefs, but they will maintain that each is equally good and true. Still others reflect an existentialist influence, declaring that theology is not of great importance; it is our spirituality and our worship which lie at the heart of each religion. They therefore minimise the significance of credal or theological differences, showing that all faiths enjoy the practice of prayer and worship. They may underline the glories of Eastern meditation, declaring that the Christian faith is inferior to Hinduism or Buddhism in this aspect of spiritual life. In one way or another they lose sight of the unique significance of the Christian Trinity, the person of Jesus Christ and his saving work on the cross and in the Resurrection.

As we shall see later, such uncritically positive approaches to other faiths have led to the situation where many in the Church deny the necessity of evangelism. They would consider it intolerant and proud to suggest that Christians should preach Jesus Christ to the faithful followers of other religions. And they would strongly oppose any Christian who actively worked to persuade people to leave their previous faith to follow Jesus Christ as Lord and Saviour.

While one fully sympathises with such Christians' reaction to the pride and apparent lack of love shown by those who dismiss other religions as demonic, we still have to ask what can lead Christians to such a naïve and unbiblical optimism concerning other faiths.

a) A personal encounter with morally upright and religiously pious followers of other faiths challenges any negative view we may previously have had about their religions. It is easy to talk about 'darkest Africa' or the 'benighted Orient' when you don't travel to those continents or meet living people from them. But when you meet pleasant and sincere Buddhists or Muslims, it becomes more difficult to dismiss their religion as purely demonic.

b) A naïve acceptance of other faiths as equally valid often stems from lack of confident faith in one's own beliefs. Historically it is clear that a belief in all religions as true has gone hand in hand with a failure to hold firm to biblical doctrines of the nature of God, revelation in the written and incarnate word, the divine-humanity of Jesus Christ, his unique atoning work on the cross, the physical resurrection of Jesus and its life-giving effect. So basic Christian doctrines are sacrificed for the sake of an easy-going tolerance of other faiths.

c) Rejection of the uniqueness of revelation and salvation in Christ can stem from a love which lacks holiness. Of course an unloving and judgmental criticism is unacceptable too. Equally we shall oppose unfair criticism of other faiths which puts up paper tigers and then shoots them down. But our love must nevertheless hold on to realistic truth which does not ignore or cover up those aspects of other religions which contradict biblical truth and deny the glory of Jesus Christ. While we must retain our critical faculties as we confess the Churches' distortions of God's revelation and our Christian failure in the moral, social and spiritual outworking of that revelation, we still affirm the absolute truth of God's word in Jesus Christ and in the Scriptures. As God's love cannot be separated from his holy judgment, so we as his children must also maintain that same balance of love and holiness. Unloving judgment may demonstrate holiness, but it is an ugly phenomenon. Unholy and uncritical love seems attractive, but it demonstrates a flabby lack of conviction and a spirit of undiscerning compromise. We all need to struggle for a true God-like love and holiness. We need to complement and help each other.

d) Christianity is Western? Troeltsch declared that to preach the superiority of Christianity over other religions meant to declare that Western culture was above all others. He equated Christianity with Western civilisation. As we have seen, past history did lead to Europe and North America becoming the heartlands and the centre of the Church. It was from them that missionaries went out to plant the Church all over the world and often the gospel was dressed in Western clothing. It is therefore understandable that people should think of the Christian faith as belonging to the West. But one is surprised at such an unsound idea being produced by a well-informed theologian. We hardly need to be reminded that the roots of the Church lie in the Middle East. Today the majority of Christians live in Asia, Africa or Latin America. One wonders therefore how Knitter can possibly support Troeltsch's assumption.

So today Troeltsch, Knitter and others still believe that the various religions have validity for their own peoples in the different parts of the world. Buddhism suits best in Japan or Thailand; Hinduism fits the Indian; Islam is the way for Arabs or Pakistanis; Judaism is the natural faith for Jews and Christianity is best for Europeans.

The Bible stands firmly against such views. The Old Testament struggles against such ideas that different gods with their religious forms belong to the various countries, that each god had his own area where he ruled. The one Creator God is Lord over all the earth and all peoples. He is made known to *all* peoples in the Messiah, Jesus of Nazareth, who died for the sin of *all* and rose to give new life to *all*.

So how do we as Christians view other religions?

3. Pluralist, Inclusivist, Exclusivist

It is customary to describe Christian attitudes to other faiths as either pluralist, inclusivist or exclusivist. Such labellings are not altogether satisfactory and more recently have come under severe attack. Furthermore each description may be placed on a spectrum of more liberal or more conservative beliefs. The three positions therefore glide into each other and it is not always easy to place any one particular Christian writer – are they really pluralist or perhaps inclusivist? Is the evangelical really exclusivist or perhaps somewhat inclusivist? Nevertheless these overall descriptions may prove helpful.

Pluralist

This position is often particularly associated with the names of John Hick and Paul Knitter. They would seem to believe that there exists some indescribable and unknowable Ultimate Absolute which may also be called the Ultimate Idea – terms which come from Hinduism. All religions with their holy books and leaders are struggling upwards towards this great Idea. Thus Christianity, the Bible and Jesus himself are searching for the elusive and unattainable goal of the Idea. The same is true of Islam, the Qur'an and Mohammed or Buddhism, the Buddha and the Dhammapada or Hinduism, the Hindu classics (the Vedas, Gita etc.), Vishnu and the other gods. All are reaching upwards towards the truth of the Idea, but none fully possesses or attains the Absolute. So Christians, Judaists and Muslims may believe that the Absolute is personal and call it/him 'God', while Buddhists, Confucianists, Taoists and many Hindus may think it is impersonal and call it Bramma, Heaven, the Tao or Brahman.

We may notice the influence of such ideas on common thought in our contemporary societies. It is now politically correct to be searching for truth, but unacceptable to claim to have found it. To be on a pilgrimage towards ultimate truth and goodness is popular, while to claim to have arrived at the source of all goodness and truth is considered arrogant.

We have then to ask what mission involves for the pluralist. Because they deny that anyone has found the Ultimate, the source of all goodness and truth, therefore it is unacceptable to aim at the conversion of others to our own faith. We learn from each other in 'dialogue' and encourage one another to be stronger in whatever faith the other person follows. Thus the Muslim should encourage the Christian to be a better Christian; the Christian should encourage the Hindu to be a more devoted Hindu etc. Conversion is considered arrogant intolerance. The pluralist is indeed tolerant of tolerance, but gravely intolerant of anything they consider intolerant.

Let me give a personal example. I was invited to speak on the subject of this book in a rather pluralistic clergy conference. The brochures introduced me as a Jewish Christian. On arrival I was drinking coffee with a minister who told me at some length about himself, his work and some of the issues he was facing. Finally he apologised for monopolising the conversation and asked me who I was. When he discovered, he immediately turned his back on me and exclaimed, 'I don't drink coffee with intolerant people'! Over his shoulder I asked him who was being intolerant – I will drink coffee with anyone. He was assuming that as a Jewish Christian I had been converted from Judaism and was therefore unaccepting of the faith of other Jews. Presuming exclusivist intolerance, he would not drink coffee with me. He was intolerant towards me because he assumed that I was arrogantly intolerant.

Inclusivist

Hans Kung, the popular Roman Catholic theologian and author, comes to mind when talking of inclusivism. As a Roman Catholic he believes in a personal God and that all religions are aiming upwards towards God. This position prevails among most Roman Catholics today and is also very influential in our societies.

Kung holds that Roman Catholics are of course highest in their pilgrimage towards God. They have the true means of grace in the Church, the true dogma, the sacraments and the hierarchy. But close behind them come the 'separated brethren', the name given to Protestants and other non-Roman Catholic Christians at the Second Vatican Council. The beliefs of such Christians contain considerable truth in agreement with the teaching of the 'true Church'. They have a form of Church, sacrament and hierarchy which resembles Roman Catholic dogma, but of course is not authentic in Kung's eyes. Nevertheless they have considerable grace in their climb towards future salvation.

Behind the 'separated brethren' come the followers of other faiths. Hindus, Buddhists and others are said by the Second Vatican Council to be very sincere in their pursuit of religious spirituality. It may be regrettable that they do not believe in the biblical God, Jesus as Saviour and Lord, the Church with its sacraments and hierarchy. But still their religious zeal places them definitely on the way towards salvation.

Indeed even humanists and Marxists will surely reach salvation, for they earnestly desire justice and social righteousness which are characteristics of the kingdom of God. So they have something of the kingdom, even if they do not have God himself. And they lack Jesus, the Holy Spirit and the Church. But salvation, inclusivists believe, will surely be theirs too.

Thus inclusivism, as also pluralism, is universalist. It believes that all will be saved. So K. Rahner in his theological dictionary has an article on Hell, in which he declares that Hell exists as a place but there will probably be no-one in it!

For the inclusivist mission may include the possibility of

people converting from a lower religion to a higher one. While this may be beneficial, it is in no way necessary for salvation. 'Dialogue' rather than evangelism still lies at the heart of mission, but conversion is now an acceptable possibility. They would consider however that preaching with the aim of converting people is unacceptable.

We may also observe that the view of salvation is firmly in the future. Little or no emphasis is placed on the past tense of salvation. Biblically however we have been saved, are being saved and look forward also to the fulness of salvation in the future.

Exclusivism

As always in discussing other faiths, the key questions relate to revelation and salvation. Does God reveal himself and his will through non-Christian religions? And can followers of other religions attain salvation apart from knowledge of and faith in Jesus Christ?

The right wing of conservative evangelicals would resist the possibility of God speaking to people of other faiths apart from knowledge of Jesus Christ and the Bible, the word of God incarnate and written. More open exclusivists remember traditional Christian theology which has always taught about general revelation (Roman Catholics call it natural revelation). Romans 1:19 declares, 'what may be known about God is plain to them, because God has made it plain to them'. God does reveal something of himself through his creation and particularly through human beings, the pinnacle of that created order. Of course this revelation is coming to us through the filter of fallen nature and is therefore marred. Also, the eye of the beholder is corrupted by sin, so the revelation is dimmed. Nevertheless, we may be assured that God does to some extent reveal himself beyond the confines of Jesus Christ and the Bible.

Can a Hindu or Buddhist be saved apart from faith in Jesus Christ? Conservative exclusivists strongly deny any such possibility, quoting well-known verses like John 14:6 or Acts 4:12.

No-one comes to the Father except through Jesus. It is only through the name of Jesus that people can be saved. At the other end of the exclusivist spectrum of belief comes the speculation that perhaps God in his grace may apply the cross and resurrection of Christ to non-Christians who would have believed if they had truly heard the gospel. Judgment remains in the hands of God. He knows the hearts of all people. But this question will be discussed more fully in the next chapter.

4. Demonic and True

It would seem that the correct Christian attitude to other religions lies in holding the two extremes in tension. An extreme negative approach does not take into account the definite truths to be found in other faiths. Likewise the uncritically positive view glosses over the falsehoods which form an integral part of these faiths. In each of the religious systems we find a combination of good and evil, beauty and ugliness, truth and untruth.

The biblical Christian has little doubt where the evil in other religions stems from. The story of the Fall in Genesis 3 shows the start of sin as a universal reality. Much as we should all love to ignore this basic truth, the facts of history compel us to acknowledge the undoubted presence of sin in us all. This not only means that all humankind falls short of God's perfect moral standards, but also that all human religious and philosophical systems contain the germ of untruth and error.

We are forced therefore to affirm that all religions and their followers are corrupted by the demonic influence of sin and untruth. It should be noted too that this must apply to all that is human in Christianity also. The Christian will therefore make an important distinction. Our biblical understanding, theology, Church practice and personal discipleship include the corrupting influence of sin and are imperfect. On the other hand God's revelation in Christ and in the Scriptures, the incarnate and the written word, remain free from sin. Every expression of the

Christian faith needs constantly to be tested by the perfect standards of God's revealed word.

Although as Christians we have little difficulty in discerning the original cause of evil and error in other faiths as well as in our own, we may find more uncertainty as to the source of truth and good outside of the specific revelation of God to his people.

Traditionally Christians have always believed in general revelation, whereby God reveals something of his character through created nature and through the human conscience. We have already observed this truth in a previous chapter, but we need to remind ourselves at this stage that this general revelation will engender some truth and goodness in all humanity and in all their religions.

In the Bible it is also clear that something of the original image of God within humankind still remains. God created us in his image and likeness with the result that by our very nature we reflect something of the character of God himself.

We maintain then that all human beings and religions combine good and evil, truth and error. Sinful and demonic influences are mitigated by the influence of general revelation and by the image of God which remains in us. But it is equally true to say that all goodness and truth in us and in our religions are corrupted by all-pervading sin and error.

Let me illustrate this truth with living examples. Some years ago I used to work in a senior approved school among criminal teenage boys. Many of them were tough and callous. And yet even the worst of them had compensating features. There was often a tremendous loyalty to their comrades and to those who befriended them. Sometimes I was amazed at the way a tough young lad would demonstrate such gentleness with a pet cat or dog.

Yes, sin is mixed with something of God in us all. Equally we have to say that even our best qualities are spoiled by sin. So my love for my wife is imperfect, for pride and selfishness are never quite defeated. My love for God too has some ulterior motives.

Even my loveliest times of prayerful worship and communion with the Lord have something of selfishness in them. I worship partly because I enjoy it and feel good as a result. I love God and believe in him not only for his sake, but also in part for what I get from him both in this life and in eternity. I have not yet attained to pure love.

Religions too share that same mixed character. Truth and error join together. For example, Islam has various aspects of its faith and practice which accord with Christian revelation. Of course we would expect this, for its foundation roots lie partly in a Jewish and Christian background. But those Jewish–Christian influences have been channelled in different directions by the animistic background and by later developments of Muslim theology.

'God is one,' Muslims affirm with sure confidence. The Christian has no hesitation in agreeing. Though Muslims may sometimes forget that the Christian belief in the Trinity in no way precludes the unity of God, actually Christians have always believed in the one Creator God. Muslims too believe in monotheism, but not a Trinitarian monotheism. So their credal statement that 'God is one' denies the Christian faith in one God, Father, Son and Holy Spirit. So the Christian agrees with the Muslim that God is indeed one, but at the same time there is a radical disagreement concerning the meaning of God's oneness.

What we have said about Islam applies equally to other religions. Judaism also has its roots firmly in the Old Testament, but it too has developed in different ways. As we have previously noted, Judaism can in no way be called a purely Old Testament faith today, for rabbinic theology maintains that God's revelation comes not only through the written Torah or Law of the Old Testament, but also through the so-called 'oral Torah'. Oral Torah consists of rabbinic teachings through the centuries which are believed to stem originally from Moses. The Talmud and other rabbinic writings contain much wisdom and truth, but the Christian would deny any claim that they are a perfect revelation from God. They too contain a mixture of truth and error. As in Islam, this may again be seen in the denial of the doctrine of the Trinity.

We have seen that human nature and all religions combine good and evil, truth and error. The same is true for human cultures. Some missionaries are strongly criticised today for their destructively negative attitude to cultures overseas. While many of the early missionary pioneers did not succumb to this temptation, some did demonstrate a cavalier disregard for the ways of other peoples. In our age we may face the opposite tendency. We sometimes join early rationalists like Rousseau in the naïve assumption that overseas cultures contain an unspoiled primitive innocence. In reaction to former negative attitudes we can be uncritically optimistic. Such a view takes little account of the biblical teaching on the universality of sin.

Actually cultures too contain a mixture of good and evil. Let me take the example of the traditional way of life among the Karo Batak people of North Sumatra. There were many lovely elements in their culture. My wife and I admired their co-operative systems of work whereby eight families shared together in working each other's fields. We were struck too by the terrific generosity which they showed not only to each other, but also to us. I would love to describe the many beautiful characteristics in Karo Batak life, but I should also mention certain weaknesses. Perhaps the most striking was the tradition that all girls at puberty had their front teeth filed down to the roots. Without any adequate pain-killing drugs the pain must have been horrific. In Karo Batak society it was also assumed that women should do all the hard work in the fields as well as look after the home and the children. The coming of the Christian faith made some significant changes in the whole culture. On the other hand much of local tradition was continued within the Church.

That is the way it should always be when the Christian faith comes into contact with other religions and cultures. The good things will be continued and hopefully refined in the life and faith of the Church. The positive elements in other cultures may also correct the biblically inadequate and culture-bound faith of the foreign missionary. Thus many Western Christian workers have found their excessively individualistic understanding of the Christian faith being broadened by the more group-conscious cultures of Africa and Asia. But error and sin will also have to be radically uprooted and replaced by positive Christian teaching and practice. This applies not only to Churches overseas, but also to Western Christians. We too need help in discerning what is essential to our faith and what comes from mere cultural tradition.

This has given rise to major debates among Christians who work among Jews and Muslims. We are having to ask what in Judaism and Islam can be carried over into the Christian life by those who come to faith in Christ from those backgrounds. But we also have to struggle boldly with the fact that some things in both religions are incompatible with faith in Jesus Christ. As Bishop Newbigin said in his books, conversion to Christ means 'radical discontinuity', but it does not mean 'total discontinuity' for there is always some continuity.

Summary

While our emotions may sweep us to extremes in our attitudes towards other cultures and faiths, we should not lose hold of the biblical teaching on general revelation and human nature. Sin and the remnant image of God interact both in cultures and religions. We dare not dismiss them as merely demonic, evil or totally false. But likewise we should not be blinded by a candy-floss tolerance which sees other faiths as equally valid as the revelation of God in Jesus Christ.

8

Is There Salvation Outside Jesus?

This is the question to elicit dogmatic answers! Is there salvation outside Jesus? The traditional evangelical Christian says 'No!' No one can find eternal life except through Jesus Christ, his death and resurrection. The more liberal Protestant will smile back with an equally dogmatic 'Yes!', despising the evangelical's insistence on traditional biblical approaches, seeing them as simplistic and intolerant. In the past, Roman Catholicism maintained that there was no salvation outside the Church, but now a much wider view holds sway. Indeed some years ago the Roman Catholic Archbishop of Boston was actually declared 'outside the Church', or excommunicate, for insisting that there was no salvation outside the Church!

While such assured dogmatism reigns in theologians' and Church leaders' statements, many ordinary Christians struggle with a deep uncertainty. Some have a vague feeling that God is much too loving to judge anyone, so there must be the hope of salvation for all. Others have been influenced by the very positive descriptions of other religions through the media and in school-teaching on comparative religion. They therefore cannot believe that God will not save through other religions just as he does through Christianity. And yet such people find it hard to square these intuitive feelings with what they have read in the Bible or heard in their younger days in Sunday School. Many evangelical Christians know the traditional teaching that salvation depends entirely on the atoning death of Christ and his life-giving resurrection. Without faith in Jesus Christ salvation is impossible. They know the key Bible texts: 'I am the way, and the truth, and the life; no man comes to the Father but by me' (John 14:6); 'there is salvation in no one else, for there is no other name under heaven given among men by which we must be saved' (Acts 4:12); 'there is one God, and there is one mediator between God and men, the man Christ Jesus' (1 Tim. 2:5) and other similar texts. But still they wonder. Is God fair to condemn people who have never heard of Jesus? Will God perhaps honour the faith and piety of the followers of other faiths? Can a loving God really judge the teeming millions of non-Christians in lands like India? When Christians were relatively isolated from other countries and faiths, it was easy to dismiss them all as in 'heathen darkness' and be confident that God would only save those who believed in Jesus Christ. But now it is different. We have met 'the heathen' and found many of them to be pleasant, sincere and goodliving. So considerable doubt underlies the evangelical affirmation that salvation is only through faith in Jesus Christ.

In looking at this whole issue we shall begin by outlining some of the suggested answers which various Christian thinkers have put forward.

1. The Cosmic Christ

Cosmic Christ theologians rightly point out that the second person of the Trinity was active in creation and in the history of humankind long before the incarnation of Jesus Christ. John's Gospel states that the pre-incarnate word of God created all things and in this word God's life gave light to all. Indeed this light 'enlightens every man' (John 1:9). Only as this first chapter of John's Gospel develops do we discover that God's word, the true light of the whole world, later became incarnate in the person of Jesus of Nazareth. The word became flesh.

Cosmic Christ theologians affirm that the Christ spirit did indeed take on flesh in the person of Jesus, but they would claim that the Christ could also be incarnate in other great religious figures. The Christ represents the activity of the High God in the world and for humanity. Wherever God works in and for the world, there the Christ is. So such theologians claim that the Christ has become incarnate in each of the great founders and saints of the various religions – Mohammed, the Buddha, Krishna or even Chairman Mao. I remember engaging in theological debate at a consultation on Communist China some years ago. My opposite number greatly admired the Chinese Communist society under Mao, for he felt that it provided the fundamental qualities of the kingdom of God – righteousness, justice and peace. While some other theologians were therefore claiming that Mao's China epitomised the kingdom of God on earth and therefore hailed Mao as the new Messiah, this theologian affirmed that the cosmic Christ was incarnate in Mao.

When asked further about the cosmic Christ in human form, my friend happily agreed that the Christ was indeed incarnate in every religious leader. When pressed he went so far as to say that actually the Christ may really be in each of us, for there is something of God active in every person of good will.

With such a theological position, universalism follows naturally. Salvation comes through faith in Christ and his work. But Christ is found in all religious leaders and indeed in all good people, so everyone, whatever his or her religion or atheistic position, will still believe in some incarnation of Christ. Christians will believe in Jesus of Nazareth as the incarnation of the Christ, Muslims in Mohammed, Buddhists in the Buddha, Communists in Marx, Lenin or Mao. Christian theologians of this persuasion will naturally emphasise the fact of God's Creation and his work in history rather than the atoning death and resurrection of Jesus Christ. Because of this lack of emphasis

on the atonement they may also underplay the fact of sin and
Satanic influences in the world. And as all humankind can find
salvation through the rich variety of incarnations of the cosmic
Christ, they see no need for the Christian to evangelise adherents
of other faiths. In fact it would be wrong to do so, for they
follow the spirit of Christ just as much as the Christian does.

Cosmic Christ theologians will readily agree to the claim
that Jesus Christ is unique, but they will want to say that other
incarnations of the Christ spirit are equally unique. We cannot
say that one is greater or better than any other.

Christians who believe in the Bible as God's special revelation
to all people will certainly want to question such cosmic Christ
theology. Although it is true that Christ, as the second person of
the Trinity, lived and was active in the world long before his
incarnation in the person of Jesus, yet the Bible clearly teaches
that Jesus is the only Son of the Father, the only sacrifice for the
sin of the world. Jesus alone is now seated at the right hand of
the Father in glory. He does not share his glory with a multitude
of other divine incarnations. Experience of other divine incarnations or emanations in no way parallels the saving effect of faith
in the person and work of Jesus Christ.

2. Anonymous Christians

The Roman Catholic theologian Karl Rahner struggled with
the issue of Christian attitudes to other religions. He came to
the idea of many in other faiths being 'anonymous Christians'.
What did he mean by that?

Rahner maintained that, 'Man must believe in God, and not
merely in God but in Christ.' But he then developed the theory
that revelation in Christ is just the final fulfilment of 'the
revelation of grace' which is found in the full acceptance of
ourselves, for God has made us to be the expression of his grace.
'The limitlessness of our transcendence', God's grace expressed
in the depths of our being, is God's revelation and word in us. In

accepting this grace and word of God within ourselves, we are actually receiving the Christ. As Rahner says, 'Anyone who does not say in his heart, "there is no God" . . . testifies to him by the radical acceptance of his being, is a believer.'

So God's grace is in us, as also in all nature. When we accept this grace in our created nature, we are accepting the Christ, God's word and activity in the world. When we accept God's grace and thus the Christ, we enter the Church, for entry into the Church is by faith in God's grace and in Christ. Of course it is true that people who accept Christ in this way may not be aware of what they are doing. They do not put a name to the Christ they are unwittingly receiving. They do not know that they have become members of the Church. They are indeed 'anonymous Christians'.

Karl Rahner's thesis has been attacked both by Christians and by the followers of other faiths. Christians have said that this distorts the Christian message, for there seems to be no biblical base for the idea of anonymous Christians. But people of other religions have accused Rahner of ecclesiastical imperialism. They claim that it is presumptuous of a Christian to label Hindus as really being Christians. The Hindu may not wish to be called a Christian, being proud of his Hindu faith. But it should be said that Rahner does believe that Christianity is the climactic and final revelation of God, so all true anonymous Christians will want to accept the full grace of God in Jesus Christ and in the Catholic Church when they hear the Christian Gospel preached in its fullness.

In his book *The Unknown Christ of Hinduism*, Panikkar quotes from Hebrews 1:1–2 saying that 'in many and various ways God spoke of old to our fathers by the prophets'. From this he deduces that the Christ has inspired not only the prophets of the Bible, but also those of Hinduism and presumably of other religious traditions also. For Panikkar, the Christ is not only the word of revelation who inspires Christian and Hindu prophets, but also the Christ is in anything which is true and good within

Hinduism. He relates the Christ to Hindu prayer and sees a possible equation between the Christ and Isvara, the personalised form of the Hindu Ultimate Absolute, Brahman. He wonders whether the Christ may be the fulfilment of the Hindus' unfulfilled longing to know Brahman. So he believes that 'we may speak not only of the unknown God of the Greeks, but also of the hidden Christ of Hinduism'.

But we have to be careful about what the New Testament really says. It does not say that salvation is through faith in some Christ spirit which is pre-incarnate. New Testament salvation is through faith in, love of and union with the incarnate Jesus of Nazareth, his historical death and physical resurrection. The Bible at no time suggests that followers of other religions might unknowingly be followers of a mystical Christ not yet incarnate.

Panikkar and Rahner speculate on the possibility that the followers of other religions are perhaps in the same position as were the Jews before the coming of Jesus Christ. We have to say however that there is a radical distinction between Old Testament religion and Hinduism, Buddhism or other non-Christian faiths. Non-Christian faiths are not intended to be just introductions to the New Testament and the person of Jesus. In fact much of their beliefs is directly opposed to the Christian faith as revealed in Jesus Christ and in the written word of the Bible, although there are elements of truth in them which will be fulfilled and perfected in Jesus Christ. The Old Testament however is aimed directly at preparing the way for the coming of the Messiah. The New Testament proclaims that Jesus fulfils the prophecies of the Old Testament and is its climax. In fact the New Testament opens with the genealogy of Jesus in Matthew 1 which specific-ally ties Jesus to the events of the Old Testament history of Israel. Jesus is the climactic pinnacle of God's revelation in Abraham, David and the exile to Babylon. Only the Old Testament prepares for Jesus the Messiah and it is he alone for whom the Old Testament prepared. The pious Jew of Old Testament times did believe in the Messiah who was to come. In no way can this be paralleled in non-Christian faiths. Hindus or Buddhists will deny that they actually believe in the Christ. They would object to being called an anonymous Christian, seeing this as just another form of Christian imperialism.

3. Christian Presence

The Protestant equivalent of the anonymous Christian approach is found in the Christian Presence school. This is represented particularly in a series of books edited by Max Warren, formerly of the Anglican Church Missionary Society.

One of this series, *Primal Vision* by John Taylor, quotes the old rabbinic question, 'Why did God speak to Moses from a thorn bush?' He then notes the rabbinic answer, 'To teach you that there is no place where the Shekinah is not.' God's glory is found even in the lowliest thorn bush.

So John Taylor deduces that God must be present and active in all religious and cultural contexts. The truth and beauty found in other faiths stems from God's work of grace in the world. And we believe that the Christ, the second person of the Trinity, is the person in the Godhead who is the agent of divine activity and revelation in the world. So Taylor would logically go on to deduce that Christ is present in other faiths and their followers. He would surely have agreed with the Russian author Tolstoy's comment, 'Where love is, God is.'

Inevitably this belief affects one's approach to mission. It can lead to a denial that Christ is in us and not in others, thus undermining the desire to go to other people in order to take Christ to them. Rather it emphasises the need to discern the Christ already present in the so-called non-Christians in order to encourage them to develop that love, faith and beauty which they are already experiencing in the other religion. The task of mission therefore consists more in listening dialogue than in verbal proclamation or preaching.

The expression 'Christian presence' implies then that Christ is present in other faiths. But it has also a second significance. Christian presence means that we as Christians must sit where others sit in order to develop what Taylor calls the 'universe of I and Thou'. The Christian is called to be present with others and engage in such a listening and loving relationship that each of us may meet the Christ in the other.

We cannot but admire the loving humility displayed by the Christian Presence school. With them we willingly confess that in our encounter with others we must be ready to 'listen to them, to understand them and to seek to be enriched by them' (M. Buber, *Writings on the Principle of Dialogue*). But as biblical Christians we cannot agree with the German Emperor Frederick the Great's view that, 'Everyone finds holiness in their own way.' In accordance with the teaching of the New Testament we affirm that Jesus Christ is God's one chosen way to bring humankind into reconciliation with himself. Christian Presence generally fails to take adequate account of the reality of human sin and rebellion. Christian mission must include worldwide evangelisation through the preaching of the Gospel of Jesus Christ.

4. Perennial Philosophy

In his *Christian Theology and World Religions,* Frank Whaling highlights the teachings of the Perennial Philosophy school. The leaders of this school come not only from the background of the Christian Church, but also from other religious traditions. Perhaps the best-known representative is the Muslim mystic scholar S. H. Nasr whose books on Islam have made a significant impression in the West.

Perennial Philosophy scholars have developed the theory of there being four levels of reality. The unmanifest, indescribable and therefore unknowable God stands at the highest level of all existence. Beneath him or it comes the manifest, describable and therefore knowable God. These first two levels in the hierarchy of existence have their parallels in the two lower levels. The higher of these is found in the invisible aspects of the world and in the mind, while the lowest level of existence is the visible and material.

We may observe the clear influence of Hindu thought on this view of reality. In non-dualist Hinduism the unknowable Brahman is the only ultimate reality. This Brahman has no attributes or characteristics – it is neither personal nor impersonal, good nor evil. Brahman can ultimately only be described by silence, for it is *Na iti, na iti*, 'Not this, not this'. The attributed and describable form of Brahman represents only an apparent and lower existence. In Christianity the mystical Hesychast movement of Eastern Orthodoxy developed something similar. It also looked for the mystical vision of the invisible essence of God which stands at the top of the ladder of knowing God through his mere activities. While it is true that ultimately the full glory of God is beyond human comprehension or vision – 'no man has ever seen or can see' the sovereign God (1 Tim. 6:16), for no-one can see God and live – yet the Bible frequently talks of people seeing and knowing God. In the New Testament, Jesus Christ so reflects the very nature and glory of God that seeing or knowing him actually means seeing or knowing God. Indeed Jesus Christ is God manifest in his glory. The Bible contradicts the Perennial Philosophy idea that the manifest and describable God represents a lower level of reality than the mystical and unmanifest divinity.

In Perennial Philosophy all religions, their scriptures, their saviours and leaders as well as their outward forms cannot attain to the highest level of unmanifest deity. As such they can all form mere stepping-stones towards the climax of mysticism with the unmanifest. All have truth, but only at a lower level. Each religion uniquely reflects the ultimate Absolute. Each shines like a different colour in the rainbow, but none can possess the fullness of Absolute Truth. S. H. Nasr therefore chides John Hick for watering down traditional Christian beliefs concerning the person of Jesus Christ. No! Let every religion give forth all the light it has and then we may be able to climb beyond them all to the ultimate Absolute, the unmanifest and so indescribable non-attributed God.

While Perennial Philosophy relates well to Eastern religious approaches, it would seem to be far removed from the standpoint of the Bible. In more recent years Western Christians have come to appreciate more mystical and less factual forms of devotion. While these can be helpful, we must not lose sight of the fundamental biblical truths of the nature of God, the Creation, the unique incarnation of Jesus Christ, his death and physical resurrection.

5. Fulfilment Theology

In the early years of the twentieth century J. N. Farquhar, a missionary in India, led the way to a new and more sympathetic appreciation of other religions, particularly Hinduism. Like some of the other movements we have been looking at, Farquhar noted elements of truth and good within Hinduism. While still believing that the Christian revelation represents the pinnacle of true religion, he came to the idea that the good in Hinduism parallels the Old Testament in leading people on towards their fulfilment in the Christian faith. For him Jesus Christ formed the crown of Hinduism, the goal of all its true aspirations. Later R. C. Zaehner developed a parallel approach. For him, too, Christ comes to fulfil all other religions. Rama and Krishna prefigure Christ, in whom 'all that has abiding value meets'.

In this approach the emphasis clearly lies in religion rather than revelation, also in the truth and goodness found in other faiths, rather than sin or the demonic. Continuity rather than discontinuity is the name of the game when the Gospel of Jesus is preached. We note the same view in Roman Catholic theology, for example in the papers of Vatican II. The good points in the various religions are charitably noted. All faiths are placed somewhere on the upward path that leads to salvation. But the assumption remains that in the Roman Catholic Church one receives more grace than elsewhere and has therefore progressed further in that salvation climb.

In seeing Jesus Christ as the crown of other faiths' dreams and the Christian revelation as the highest, this differs radically from the theology of such theologians as Cantwell Smith, John Hick and Paul Knitter. The latter would rather maintain that there is some higher God or Ultimate Absolute beyond the particular beliefs of all religions, including Christianity. In this they resemble the Perennial Philosophy school, but they do not hold the mystical idea that the unmanifest is higher than the manifest. They affirm that all religions are true for their own followers, but no religion has universal truth. So Knitter dismisses the uniqueness of Jesus Christ as just the early disciples' expression of love. A child may lovingly declare that their father is the best in the world and may really believe it. The disciples, too, proclaimed Jesus as the only redeemer and Son of the Father. So the Christian faith and the Bible are true for the believer, but not for others.

Whether other religions are fulfilled in Jesus Christ as their crown or whether all religions find their fulfilment in some higher divine form, in any case there is no radical distinction between the faith of Christ and other religions. It is significant that all these theologians talk little of sin and even less of God's judgment. They seem far removed from the Japanese theologians K. Kitamori and K. Koyama with their emphasis on God's pain because of human sin and God's wrath which demonstrates God's personal dynamic activity in history.

I applaud fulfilment theology's desire to take other faiths seriously and show a loving attitude. I wholeheartedly agree with their teaching that there is truth, goodness and beauty in other religions, as we have already observed. Those elements of goodness should indeed find their perfect fulfilment in the glory of Jesus Christ, but these theologians have taken inadequate account of the sin and untruth within other religions. Because of these corrupt elements a radical break is required when entering into faith in Jesus Christ. Entry into his kingdom always necessitates repentance and conversion.

6. What of the Future?

One day I received a letter from a Muslim objecting to a book I had written entitled *Islam and Christian Witness.* The writer detailed the horrors of hell towards which I was heading. He knew the exact number of scorpion and snake bites to which I would be subjected. The long list of other tortures filled several pages. But then he turned to the delights that awaited me if I repented – how many beautiful maidens would serve me and how many golden goblets of wine would refresh me. Having read through these lengthy descriptions of heaven and hell I smiled. Such a naïve letter was hardly likely to frighten or entice into repentance.

In Western cultures today we have largely lost interest in the after-life. We have reacted against our forefathers' preaching of hell with all its lurid descriptions of judgment. And we are generally more interested in the fullness of life now in this world than pie in the sky when we die. In other areas of the world, however, many people retain a vivid concern for heaven and fear of hell. For example, in many Chinese circles young people have been deeply impressed by horrific pictures of the agonies of hell displayed at funerals. In my experience among Chinese people, many are converted to Jesus Christ because he promises eternal life and freedom from the threat of hell.

But what do we mean by heaven and hell?

The Bible seems to imply that the after-life is a heightening and continuation of our present experience. What we are now, we shall be fully. If we know and love God now, we shall find the full knowledge and love of God in eternity. If we delight to praise and worship the Lord now, the Book of Revelation describes heaven as God on the throne with the multitudes of his people praising and worshipping him. If we have entered his kingdom by new birth and begun the kingdom life of righteousness, justice and peace, then in the after-life we shall experience the new heaven and the new earth where these characteristics flourish fully. Our present joy in the Lord will be complete – and there will be no more sin, tears and distress. As the Chinese theologian C. S. Song has beautifully said, all the present is caught up into the resurrection future.

In the Bible, Jerusalem stands for the focal point of the whole people of God. This city of peace represented the very presence of God in the midst of his people. It was also the centre of worship, for God dwelt in the temple there. All the people thought of pilgrimage to the holy city as the high point of their life, the greatest time of joyful community with other worshippers. No wonder the glory of heaven is described in the Bible as the heavenly city, the new Jerusalem. But we may need to be careful in the use of such pictorial language. The Kenyan theologian, John Mbiti, points out that to most Africans the city is the place of secular materialism and greed to which men go without their wives or families in order to make money which they can then take back to their village. The city is a lonely place, a centre of temptation and sin. The ideal rests in the *shamba*, the homestead and fields in the village. At home there is family unity, loving communication and peace. Heaven is more a new *shamba* than a new city! Whatever picture of heaven we may use, we still understand it as the ideal fulfilment of all that is good in the present.

Loving communication in unity together lies at the heart of biblical ideals. In the picture of the original Garden of Eden, Adam, Eve and God could share intimately together without inhibitions. Sin breaks such communication. Heaven is the fullness of loving union with God himself when God's people

131

stand together in the fullness of worship. In heaven we shall know and love perfectly.

But what about hell? One shudders even to write about it. How one wishes that no such judgment existed! Doffing his cap to traditional dogma, one leading Roman Catholic writer has suggested that hell exists, but probably it remains empty! Would that he might be proved correct! Sadly, however, Jesus has warned us that few find the narrow gate which leads to life while many take the easy way which leads to destruction. As in Matthew 7:13–14 so also in John's Gospel there seems to be a clear contrast between perishing and life. But both have eternal consequences. Those who believe in Jesus shall gain eternal life; those who reject him shall perish because 'the wrath of God rests upon him' (John 3:36).

Popular views of hell often owe more to legend and medieval art than to biblical reality. Such vivid pictorial images of torture and torment may frighten some into surrender to God, but they engender a false view of the character of God and will surely repel all sensitive and thoughtful people. While we must take serious account of God's absolute holiness and burning purity, he is not a vindictive God who enjoys wreaking vengeance on unbelievers.

Hell is rather to be seen as a serious affirmation of the moral nature of the universe which was created with purposes of holiness by a God of righteousness. It witnesses to the God-given human responsibility of moral choice and freedom.

Hell would seem to represent the climax to a life apart from God in Christ. If today we are separated from God by our sin and stand under his judgment, then hell is the natural conclusion of such a course. Hell lacks all true relationship or communication – and we see all too clearly the seeds of that tragedy in the world around us.

In the Bible we note again and again how judgment and salvation go closely together as the two sides of the one coin. This is because God's nature includes both loving grace and also absolute holiness which cannot tolerate sin. Today it is more fashionable to talk about the loving kindness of our God than about his holiness. We therefore find it hard to accept that God could condemn anyone in righteous judgment.

7. Salvation by Jesus Christ Alone?

It is customary among some theologians today to disregard the fundamentals of biblical revelation and of the traditional teachings of the Christian Church throughout the last two thousand years. For example Paul Knitter supports those fellow theologians who dismiss the incarnation as just a myth. He then says 'they avoid the incredible (for many) and exclusivistic understanding of Jesus as a pre-existent divine being who comes down from heaven, takes on a human nature (without a human personality), does his work of redeeming, and then goes back to heaven'. He goes on to declare that 'such a literal understanding tends not only to dehumanise Jesus, but so to humanise God as to confine deity to Jesus'. Having thus caricatured traditional Christian theological positions, he then castigates them as 'excesses'.

If with Knitter we deny the deity of Christ as the second person of the Trinity, his incarnation, his divine-human person, his redeeming work on the cross, his resurrection and ascension, then of course we are no longer talking of the truth revealed in the Bible nor of the faith of the Church throughout Christian history. However we may call our new religious concoction 'Christianity', it actually has little relationship to the Christian faith. We have in fact invented a new religion which has changed or denied every major point in the Christian faith.

If we no longer accept Jesus Christ's deity, incarnation or atoning work through the cross and resurrection, then of course little remains that marks Christianity out as unique and radically different from other faiths. We can only stand amazed at the boldness and pride of Christians who dismiss as inadequate or even untrue the fundamentals of the Christian faith which godly and intelligent Christian scholars have believed throughout the past two thousand years. They evidently know better than all who went before them. And yet they can accuse traditional Christians of arrogance. Before we ask the question, therefore, whether salvation is by Jesus Christ alone, we have first to reaffirm our faith in the basic truths revealed in the Bible and to which the Church has witnessed all through its history. In this book we are not in a position to defend these truths against the attacks of more liberal theologians, but we want to declare again our faith. We believe in the triune God, Father, Son and Holy Spirit. We stand firm on the biblical revelation of God's word to all people to determine the content of our faith and the quality of our lives. This word judges us as to whether we remain faithful to God in our beliefs and in our lives. We reaffirm the words of the Christian creed that Jesus Christ, God's only Son, was 'born of the Virgin Mary'. Knowing the tragic reality of universal sin, we rejoice in Jesus Christ's redeeming death for the sin of the world. We have experienced something of the glorious freedom from guilt and from the stain of sin which God gives to all who believe in his Son, Jesus Christ. We are also encouraged by God's gift to us of new life in the resurrection of Jesus. We have begun to know a little of the work of the Holy Spirit in changing our lives, giving us his fruit (Gal. 5:22) in order to make us more like our Lord and imparting to us gifts to enable us to serve him and our world. And we look forward with confident hope to the fullness of eternal life which awaits all believers in Jesus Christ.

When we list these fundamentals of the Christian faith, we cannot but exclaim with wonder, 'Hallelujah!' No other faith or religion can match the glory of such biblical realities. But we confess with deep sadness that neither our lives nor our culture-bound preaching have allowed the light of the gospel to shine in its full beauty.

The central feature of the biblical gospel is the death and resurrection of Jesus Christ. The four Gospels in their life histories of Jesus concentrate on his death and resurrection. His life and his teaching points forward to this climax. John records how Jesus called the utter humiliation of the cross 'my glory' and 'my hour'. This is God's chosen way to deal with the horror of sin which afflicts every people and every person. Jesus alone is God's sacrificial Lamb who has died for the sins of the world. And he alone has been raised from the dead by the Father to give new life to all who will put their faith in him. He is truly unique in his redeeming and atoning death, as also in his life-giving resurrection.

What about good non-Christians?

In the Old Testament prophets God judges the nations not only for their idolatry and religious sin, but particularly for their moral failure and cruelty to others. For example in Habakkuk 2:6–17, the Chaldeans are condemned for plundering other peoples, pride and drunkenness, but then also Habakkuk mentions briefly their sin of idolatry (Hab. 2:18,19). This may be paralleled in other prophetic writings, including Isaiah who foresees God's destruction of Babylon the oppressor (Isa. 14:4) because she 'smote the peoples in wrath' (Isa. 14:6), and because of her 'pomp' (Isa. 14:11). But the Old Testament consistently stresses that religion and ethics go together. True worship of God must include righteousness and justice. Idolatry and moral corruption also go hand in hand. So God judges people for moral and religious sin together. The New Testament teaches us that all people fall short of God's standards of holiness, all are sinners (Rom. 3:23). In talking of 'good non-Christians' therefore, we are using comparative terms. In comparison with other people some may be considered 'good', but in comparison with the glory of God 'all our righteous deeds are like a polluted garment' (Isa. 64:6). Human merit is never adequate to earn God's favour. In this context the Gospel of Jesus Christ shines out as good news indeed. Christians will long to share the good news with all the world. While we can deduce the fundamental elements of the gospel we are called to preach from the New Testament, we cannot be quite so sure how much of our message people need to receive before they can be saved. Judgment belongs to God, not to us. It behoves us to stay humble when talking about God's final judgment. By his grace we can and should know for sure whether *we* have eternal life (1 John 5:13), but only God knows the heart of other people. Our task remains to share with all people the fullness of the good news of Jesus Christ.

Despite the long history of Christian persecution of Jews, which climaxed in the cataclysmic horror of the holocaust, we are encouraged today to find that increasing numbers of thinking Jews are asking questions about Jesus of Nazareth. 'He is part of our Jewish history,' some are saying, 'and we have somehow got to fit him in.' Who was this Jesus really? What did he do? How does he fit into our national and religious history? Some Orthodox Jews have begun to write books examining the evidence concerning the life of Jesus. One or two have even accepted the Virgin Birth and the physical resurrection of Jesus – it is a strange paradox when some Christian leaders reject these fundamentals of the Christian faith while some Orthodox Jews can accept them! But they still reject his claims to be God incarnate and they do not believe that he died on the cross as our sin-bearer.

Some Muslims too have a deep love for Jesus, although they firmly reject any suggestion that he is God. The idea that Jesus died on the cross is also anathema to them. I remember one Sufi Muslim declaring to me with enthusiasm, 'When you see Jesus, you see God.' But without faith in Jesus as Lord and sin-bearing Saviour could he be saved? Such an incident leads us to ask ourselves at what stage of their pilgrimage Jesus' twelve disciples received eternal life. Was it when they first followed Jesus although they still had no idea of his future death on the cross and his resurrection? And at that early stage did they realise that Jesus was God incarnate?

It was said of Keshab Chandra Sen, the leader of Reform Hinduism, that he loved Jesus more than any other. He wanted his life to be patterned on Jesus. But his knowledge of the Christian Church in its Westernised forms of life and teaching left him cold. The doctrine of the Trinity also formed a particular stumbling-block which prevented him becoming a Christian.

We know from the Bible that the message of salvation must include Jesus Christ as Lord and Saviour. We know that the gospel is centred on the fundamental facts of Jesus' death for our sin and his life-giving resurrection. We long that all people everywhere should know and receive the gospel of Jesus in its fullness. We can only speculate whether perhaps God in his amazing grace may save some whose knowledge of the gospel is gravely deficient, but yet they may believe in Jesus, love and follow him.

In his writings Professor Norman Anderson, the Christian theologian and Islamicist, suggests the possibility that God may save some on the grounds of their humble repentance and faith in God. In this he denies the possibility that they should be saved because of their religious piety, for the Bible clearly rejects any idea of salvation through good works or merit. He is therefore not suggesting at all that anyone is saved on the basis of their religious sincerity. But perhaps God may apply the saving work of Jesus Christ to those who have a humble and repentant faith which looks to God for his gift of eternal life by grace. They may never have heard of Jesus but God still may apply the shed blood of Christ to such people. We realise of course that such ideas remain in the realm of speculation and cannot be proved by Scripture. But again we have to remind ourselves that God is the judge; we are not. We know that he will always remain righteous and just in all his judgments, but we cannot know in detail how he works out his justice.

It seems that there may be one other possible way of salvation in Christ for those who have never heard of Jesus Christ. We realise that it was to his disciples that Jesus promised 'seek, and you will find' (Matt. 7:7), but he goes on to apply this promise to '*everyone* . . . who seeks'. How may this prove true for those who have never heard of Jesus Christ? I am interested how often one hears missionary stories of men and women who have earnestly and humbly sought eternal life and then have seen a vision or received a dream. Again and again they have seen the figure of Jesus in their dream or vision. Some have even been told that his name is Jesus. I think of a man who had never even heard of the Christian religion, but he was given a vision in which he saw a man dressed in white with holes in his hands. Such visions and mystical experiences can have a lasting life-changing impact on the person concerned, but cannot be the basis for preaching to others because they have no objective base. But can we recognise such stories as one of God's means to keep his promise that those who seek will find?

I have tentatively suggested some possibility of salvation outside of the normal route of hearing the good news of Jesus Christ and so coming to faith in him. We must reiterate the fact that such suggestions remain mere speculation. And we know that in all cases salvation can only come on the grounds of the atoning death of Jesus Christ. According to the Bible certain facts remain unassailably true. Firstly, salvation comes to us by grace through repentance and faith in Jesus Christ, his death and resurrection. Secondly, in the New Testament, salvation comes to sinners, not to those who feel confident in their own faith or righteousness. L. Newbigin points out in this context that the New Testament emphasis 'is always on surprise' (*The Open Secret*, p. 196). While it is true that in the final judgment God will doubtless surprise many humble sinners by his saving grace, we have also to note that people who believe in Jesus Christ should have a humble assurance that they have eternal life (1 John 5:13).

9

Dialogue and/or Proclamation?

We have observed that all religions contain a bewildering combination of truth and error, good and evil, light and darkness. The demonic corrupts the image of God which remains in humankind. How then should Christians relate to other faiths?

Our emphasis concerning other faiths will inevitably affect our approach to them. If we overplay the truth and goodness in other religions and neglect to take note of the demonic corruption of truth in them, then we shall of course deny the need for their followers to be converted to Christ. If sin and error play only a minor role in the drama, then the redeeming work of Jesus Christ on the cross will also not feature significantly. The emphasis of the Christian may then lie heavily on a form of dialogue which listens and learns, but does not preach the good news of Jesus Christ with the aim that people should be converted to him.

If on the other hand we underline the Satanic source of all non-Christian religions and highlight their evil and untruth, then we may be prone to an arrogant, unlistening preaching of the gospel which only demands a radical repentance and new birth.

In the jargon of mission thinking today we talk of continuity and discontinuity. Because some elements of truth persist in other faiths and in all pre-Christian religious life, the Christian faith builds on the sound foundation it finds there. The Christian preacher should seek out those points in non-Christian thought which can act as bridges into the fullness of Christian truth. Then the full beauties of biblical revelation and the glory of Jesus Christ by the Spirit will cleanse and fulfil what is carried over into the new believer's Christian faith. There must always be some continuity between other faiths and Christian life and belief.

But this emphasis on continuity must not be divorced from the equally necessary fact of discontinuity. When Jesus Christ becomes our Lord and Saviour, we cannot allow the demonic to remain. When Jesus Christ reigns as lord in our lives and takes central place in our beliefs, he will not share his throne with Satan, untruth or evil. Conversion to Jesus Christ demands a radical repentance which renounces Satan and all his works. We are called upon to turn from all other gods and all beliefs and practices which are not consonant with the biblical revelation. And even as Christians we need constantly to repent of the untruth and sin which continually distort our faith.

Because all human religion permits truth and error to co-exist, continuity and discontinuity must hold hands together in the new life in Jesus Christ. But is that equally true of dialogue and proclamation? Before we jump to conclusions we need to examine what we mean by these two key words.

1. Dialogue

In our contemporary world this word 'dialogue' is used so frequently that we sometimes forget that it requires some definition. It is more than possible that we may use the word without actually having any clear sense of what it means.

a) Not monologue

Dialogue is often contrasted with a form of preaching which does not attempt to understand or learn from the other person. Such preaching lacks loving personal attitudes in what Martin Buber called the 'I–Thou' relationship. It frequently treats the other person as a mere object of evangelisation – what Buber called an 'I–It' relationship. So dialogue may be defined as a form of communication which does not only indulge in a monologue declaration of the gospel. Dialogue must include the opportunity for all involved to share their beliefs and feelings. This means that dialogue always takes the form of a discussion or debate rather than a one-sided proclamation which allows no sharing, questioning or disagreement from the listener. The Sunday sermon from most pulpits remains in most churches the most obvious example of a form of communication which is not dialogue.

In his *Dialogue with the World*, J. G. Davies accuses such monologue forms of preaching or teaching of being 'entirely lacking in humility'. There must be a considerable danger of pride in such one-sided preaching. We can so easily fall into the trap of feeling that we alone have all the truth with nothing to learn from anyone else. We then come to believe that our understanding of God's revealed truth is already perfect and needs no further correction or growth. All of us would want immediately to denounce such attitudes of pride. None of us actually would really feel that we have achieved such perfection, although our form of preaching may suggest such an impression to our listeners; indeed, our form of monologue preaching may actually lead us towards such unspoken attitudes of pride.

Later we shall note that both Jesus and his apostles did sometimes engage in direct monologue preaching, so there must be the possibility of this activity being without arrogant pride. In fact we could all cite examples of people we know who preach and teach in monologue style, but do so with deep humility.

In his earlier book *Sandals at the Mosque*, Kenneth Cragg argues that dialogue in the sense of a reverent, tactful, tender and sensitive approach is not merely to be argued for 'on a tactical score', but also because it reflects a genuine and humble concern for the other person. If our manner of preaching does not convey a Christ-like love and humility, then our lives actually preach a false gospel even if our words remain utterly biblical.

Our first definition of the word 'dialogue' is that it takes the form of mutual discussion and debate rather than just a monologue proclamation.

b) Learning from others

In the Keele Evangelical Anglican Congress, dialogue was defined as a situation where, 'Each party . . . desires to listen and learn as well as to speak and instruct.' Listening and learning certainly constitute a vital part of dialogue. Indeed some advocates of dialogue stress listening and learning to the neglect of any speaking and instructing. So it has been said that we all choose either compassion or jabbering. If we preach or teach, they say, we merely engage in jabbering. But if we remain silent in order to learn from the other, then we show compassion. Even Roger Hooker in his book *Outside the Camp*, advocates the silence of listening by commending Job's comforters for their first seven days and nights with Job when they kept silent. He suggests that they fell into error when they began to instruct Job verbally.

We have then to ask, how far is it right that the Christian should learn from other faiths and their followers? Humility compels us to affirm that we have much to learn from all sources. We dare not stand with rigid pride, declaring that others have nothing to teach us. On the other hand we may feel threatened by the suggestion that as biblical Christians we can still learn from other religions. This might suggest to us that the Christian revelation in the Bible and in Jesus Christ needs further instruction and perfecting at the hands of other faiths. Faith in the absolute all-sufficiency of the Christian revelation seems to conflict with the moral pressures of gracious humility. Do we then need to learn from other faiths?

It seems to me that this question requires us to make a fundamental distinction between revelation and theology. As Christians we believe that God's revealed word is the truth. We maintain that God has given us a perfect revelation in his written word, the Bible, and particularly in his incarnate word, Jesus Christ. We cannot accept that Mohammed, Krishna or the Buddha have anything significant to add to Jesus Christ and they cannot in any way correct him. Likewise we do not accept that the Qur'an, the Vedas or the Buddhist scriptures can be God's instrument to perfect or correct the Bible.

On the other hand the Christian Church's human attempts to understand and interpret God's revelation fall far short of perfection. All theology, including even the Church's credal statements, requires correction and perfecting. All of us as Christians must sense the fearful inadequacy of our under-standing of God's word, let alone our personal relationship with the Lord and with our neighbour. We need all the help we can get from almost any source to rebuke, challenge, teach and push us forwards in our growth as Christians.

Paul Knitter tells us that as Christians we need to learn from Islam the emphasis that God is one, from Hinduism their concept of non-duality and from Eastern religions generally the practice of personal contemplation and acting without seeking the fruits of one's actions. But surely all of these points are to be found in perfect form within the teachings of the Bible? Nevertheless we may as Christians need to be reminded of such biblical truths and corrected in our misunderstandings or in our neglect of them. While we may affirm without hesitation that the Bible teaches clearly that God is one, many of us may actually slip into a careless tritheism in the way we talk of and relate to the three persons of the Trinity. With regard to Hindu non-duality we might wish to question their understanding that 'all is Brahman', for it denies the ultimate existence and worth of the created order and of humankind. We shall also want to underline the biblical doctrine of our union with Christ and thus with God the Father. Nevertheless we are grateful that Hinduism challenges us to remember a truth which we sometimes may forget or neglect. And we are glad that Hinduism challenges us to rethink just what we actually mean by our union with God. Likewise the Eastern religious emphasis on meditation is in no way alien to biblical teaching, for often in the Bible we are exhorted to wait on the Lord and to be quiet in his presence as we wait for him to speak to us. And we shall want to stress that Christian concepts of meditation must be affirming of the reality of ourselves and of the whole created order, so we cannot simply accept Eastern meditation with its aim of self-emptying or of contemplating the spirit within. Nevertheless we have to confess that as Christians we have often become too verbose and we have forgotten the art of quiet meditation. In former centuries the monks and desert fathers were strong in such matters, but more recently we have often been guilty of losing this emphasis. In these days we are learning much from Eastern religious meditation despite its inherent dangers to a Christ-centred faith.

When we truly encounter other religions and genuinely seek to walk in their sandals, we begin to observe our own biblical faith and our theological traditions through different spectacles. As Frank Whaling says (*Christian Theology and World Religions*), 'It is necessary in some degree to see the world through *their* eyes in the light of *their* questions as they emerged in *their* history.' At present most of us see God's revelation through the lens of a Western worldview, Western theological and Church tradition. How helpful therefore to be forced by other traditions to re-examine our understanding and practice of the Christian faith!

The infinite God in all his glorious holiness and splendour remains far beyond anything we have grasped or attained to, so we always have much to grapple with in his revelation of himself in his word. We are deeply grateful for anything which stimulates us to grow in our knowledge of the Lord.

To summarise this section, we maintain that God's revelation in his incarnate and written word is perfect, in no way deficient. It needs no correcting or perfecting at the hands of other religions. But our human attempts to understand, formulate and practise the biblical faith of Jesus Christ are distinctly fallible and imperfect. In dialogue with followers of other religions we may well learn much and grow in our faith.

c) Dialogue dangers

In official inter-religious dialogue there is a tendency only to invite participants who share a belief that Christians should not preach with the aim of conversion to Jesus Christ. A friend of mine who is intimately involved in dialogue with representatives of the Jewish community has shared with me some of his experiences. He has found that the Jewish participants in the dialogue have not been happy with Christian evangelism, but they have realised that obedience to Jesus Christ and the New Testament requires Christians to proclaim the good news of Jesus as Messiah and Saviour. They have therefore been open to friendly relationships with my friend despite his commitment to evangelism among Jews. Sadly, however, he has not found equal acceptance among the other Christian participants in the dialogue.

It is also rare that such dialogue groups will include in their ranks any Christians who have been converted from Judaism. Likewise former Muslims will not normally be allowed to share in such discussions. It is not only in dialogue teams that the Church generally fails to include Jewish Christians. The advisory committee on Jewish–Christian questions for the 1988 Lambeth Conference for Anglican Bishops invited non-Christian Jews to participate, but failed to allow any Jewish Christian to play a part. One would have thought that Jewish Christians should have played a primary role in advising the Church on Jewish–Christian issues!

Christian dialogue teams have tacitly agreed that the Christian Church is fundamentally a Gentile movement and therefore Jews ought not to be converted to become followers of Jesus as Messiah. Some Christian theologians like Paul Van Buren have spelled this out, maintaining that Judaism is God's way for Jews while Christianity has become the faith for European Gentiles. Such an approach denies the universality of the Christian faith and can make the Church racially exclusive. He lays down three conditions as foundational for dialogue. While his first condition demands that all participants should have a firm religious faith based on 'an encounter with the holy', his second insists that we should recognise possible truth in all religions and that this truth is 'grounded in the hypothesis of a common ground and goal for all religions'. We have already argued that there is indeed truth in all faiths, but the biblical Christian will find it impossible to agree that all religions stand on common ground and are directed at the same goal. Indeed, even if we do not accept his rejection of natural theology, we need to take seriously Karl Barth's declaration that human religions represent not so much humankind's search for God, but rather a move away from God. Paul in Romans 1 also seems to see in the history of human religion a spiritual degeneration, not a positive God-ward evolution. Nevertheless, by the grace of God it is true that God sometimes speaks to people in the context of their religious life and practice – or should we rather say that God sometimes speaks to us despite our religion? Van Buren's third condition for dialogue is that we should be open to the possibility of being converted to the other religion. Of course it is true that none of us 'possess the final, definitive, irreformable truth', so of course we are open to learn and even to be rebuked for our errors. But we still cannot abandon our firm conviction that God has revealed to us himself and his salvation in the person and work of Jesus Christ. If dialogue demands that we weaken our faith in our Lord Jesus, then such dialogue can only be rejected.

Van Buren also maintains that the goal of dialogue is to make 'the Christian a better Christian and the Buddhist a better Buddhist'. In this he joins the growing stream of theologians who reject the universality or catholicity of the Church. He agrees with the Roman Catholic theologian Karl Rahner that the Early Church was 'the Jewish–Christian Church', but that gave birth to the narrower 'Western Church'. Although he looks forward to the day when the Church will again 'become a truly World Church', he somehow feels this will be achieved by encouraging people of all faiths towards a deeper grasp of God's truth within their own religion. But is this really the aim of true mission and dialogue?

Those of us who believe in the authority of Scripture will want to examine the use of the words for 'dialogue' in the New Testament and the apostolic practice of dialogue as recorded for us in the Acts of the Apostles.

d) 'Dialogue' in the New Testament

I have already observed in my book *Islam and Christian Witness*, that the New Testament uses three variations of the Greek word for dialogue and does so with clear significance.* *Dialogizomai* and the related *dialogismos* seem to have the sense of questioning and uncertain thinking, while *dialegomai* has the much more definite idea of arguing, reasoning and contending. In his Gospel, Luke only uses the uncertain and questioning *dialogizomai* and *dialogismos*, while in the Acts of the Apostles he changes

---

*Kenneth Cracknell in his *Towards a New Relationship* notes the New Testament use of *dialegomai* and *dialogizomai*, but states that both 'have the force of "to argue", "to reason", "to contend" '. Cracknell also fails to observe that Luke carefully changes in his vocabulary from the words used in his Gospel to that used in the Acts of the Apostles. *Dialegomai* occurs in Acts 17:2,17; 18:4,19; 19:8,9; 20:7,9; 24:12,25 – also in Mark 9:34; Hebrews 12:5, Jude 9. *Dialogizomai* occurs in Luke 1:29; 3:15; 5:21,22; 12:17; 20:14 – also in Matthew 16:7,8; 21:25; Mark 2:6,8; 8:16,17; 9:33; John 11:50. *Dialogismos* occurs in Luke 2:35; 5:22; 6:8; 9:46,47; 24:38 – also in Matthew 15:19; Mark 7:21; Romans 1:21, 14:1; 1 Corinthians 3:20; Philippians 2:14; 1 Timothy 2:8; James 2:4.

to *dialegomai* to demonstrate the confident preaching of the apostles.

In Luke's Gospel the dialogue word *dialogizomai* is used when Mary is bewildered by the coming of the Angel Gabriel. Mary 'dialogued' in her mind concerning the angel's greeting (Luke 1:29). In Luke 5:21–22 the RSV rightly translates the word for dialogue as 'questioning'. The scribes and Pharisees questioned in their hearts about Jesus' claim to be able to forgive sins. In every case Luke's usage of this word demonstrates a deep uncertainty and questioning, not an assured faith to be proclaimed.

When the apostle Paul uses this same word, he too conveys a negative uncertainty which he sees as an expression of empty futility. So in Romans 1:21 Paul shows the sin of the Gentiles who had become 'futile in their "dialoguing" and their senseless minds were darkened'. Again in 1 Corinthians 3:20 he denounces 'dialoguings of the wise' as futile. In fact Paul never speaks positively about the practice of 'dialogue'. The apostle James also describes such 'dialogue' as 'evil' (Jas. 2:4).

But when Luke turns to the missionary activity of the apostles, he carefully avoids the forms of the word for dialogue used in his Gospel. Now he uses only *dialegomai* and this has quite a different feel.

Advocates of dialogue commonly refer to the Acts of the Apostles 17 as a supporting text. The word for dialogue appears twice in this chapter (Acts 17:2; 17) and in both cases the RSV translates it as 'argued'. Kenneth Cracknell is surely right to point out that Paul's witness took place in the synagogue. As he says, Christians today so often want to present their message in a church or Christian home where they feel safe and on home territory. But Paul argued his case in the synagogue where the other Jews felt at home and could set the agenda for the discussion. This is equally true of Paul's 'dialogues' in the Acts of the Apostles 18:4,19 and 19:8. So also in the daily dialogues in the hall, or school, of Tyrannus (Acts 19:9) those present could probably determine the issues to be debated.

But we notice in the Acts of the Apostles how the word 'dialogue' is clearly linked to the proclamation of the word of God, the good news of Jesus Christ. And Paul aims unhesitatingly for the conversion of men and women to Jesus Christ. So in 17:2 the content of his dialogue is 'from the scriptures, explaining and proving that it was necessary for the Christ to suffer and to rise . . .' He concludes by declaring that, ' "this Christ, whom I proclaim to you, is the Christ" '. The result was that some believed, while others angrily 'set the city in an uproar' (Acts 17:5). We can hardly imagine modern ecumenical dialogues producing such definite reactions!

What then shall we conclude from the apostolic practice of dialogue as shown to us in the Acts of the Apostles? We may draw four conclusions:

i) Apostolic dialogue may often use debate rather than just monologue preaching. But it does not always do so. The Acts of the Apostles contains several of the apostles' evangelistic sermons in which there is a definite preaching without using dialogue debate as the method (e.g. Stephen's sermon in Acts 7; Paul's preaching in Acts 13:16–41, 17:22–31). Sometimes the apostle Paul also taught at such length in monologue fashion that a young man 'sank into a deep sleep as Paul talked still longer'! As a result he fell out of the window!

ii) Apostolic dialogue contains a definite message to proclaim. The apostles never contented themselves with mere discussion, but always preached a clear-cut gospel. They did not merely share their respective religious experience, as often happens in modern dialogue, but rather they preached Jesus, his death and his resurrection. John Stott says in his *Christian Mission in the Modern World*, 'Paul's dialogue was clearly a part of his proclamation and subordinate to his proclamation.'

iii) Apostolic dialogue always aims for the conversion of others to Jesus Christ. When one reads the Acts of the Apostles it is inconceivable that the apostles would have encouraged their fellow Jews just to become better Judaists, or the Gentiles to become more dedicated followers of their gods. No! The apostles longed for both Jews and Gentiles to turn in repentance and faith to Jesus Christ as Saviour and Lord.

iv) Apostolic dialogue may take place where non-Christians are on home territory and can force Christians to relate their preaching to the questions and issues that are relevant to people outside the Church. The apostles proclaimed the gospel in the world, not just in the Church.

e) Jesus and the apostles

It is evident that both Jesus and the apostles had done their homework concerning the current beliefs and philosophies around them. They did not preach and teach in ignorance. Over the years they must have studied and listened in order to have gained such a grasp of contemporary worldviews.

Jesus himself began his education while still young. Luke records that as a boy of twelve Jesus sat among the teachers in the temple 'listening to them and asking them questions' (Luke 2:46). In typical Jewish fashion the teachers taught partly by asking questions, so Jesus not only listened but also gave answers. We read that 'all who heard him were amazed at his understanding and his answers' (Luke 2:47).

It would seem that Jesus did not begin his public ministry until he reached the age of thirty. He therefore had considerable time to develop his knowledge of the Old Testament and also of the traditional writings and teachings of the rabbis. So we are not surprised that the very first public ministry recorded for us is based on Scripture (Luke 4:16–27). This passage shows that Jesus already had a good understanding of the section from Isaiah which he was asked to read in the synagogue that Sabbath morning. Then the people wondered why he only read the words about God's grace and omitted the later verses in Isaiah 61 concerning God's judgment on the Gentiles. Jesus then demonstrated again his knowledge of the Old Testament. He reminded his hearers how Elijah only fed the Gentile widow from Zarephath, not someone from Israel. Likewise Elisha only healed the Gentile Naaman from Syria, not one of the many Jewish lepers.

We also find that Jesus knew the traditional teachings of the rabbis. His own words often relate directly to them and so to contemporary debates. For example, Jesus' teaching about the kingdom of God clearly refers to current views on this subject. Likewise what he has to say about the sabbath, divorce and many other topics.

Over the years Jesus had evidently listened and learned to good effect. He understood how people felt and what they believed. His teaching built on this good foundation.

The apostles followed in their master's footsteps. They too had studied and learned before they preached and taught. Particularly for Paul, the apostle to the Gentiles, his field of learning needed to be wide. He often preached in Jewish synagogues, so he needed to know the same areas of study that Jesus had learned. Paul was required to have a good grasp of Jewish thought. In fact he had studied under the great Jewish rabbi Gamaliel and he was steeped from his youth in the whole atmosphere of pious Jewish life. But then his ministry carried him into the Gentile world of Greek philosophy and religion. We cannot but be impressed therefore when we find him quoting Greek poets, prophets and philosophers (e.g. Acts 17:22–31; Titus 1:12). He seems to have known the context into which he was preaching and therefore his message came with evident relevance.

In relating his Hebrew message to Gentiles in the Greek language, Paul was compelled to adapt the content of the gospel to a new philosophical context. His letter to the Colossians gives us a superb example of how he takes over and bends to his own use both the vocabulary and thought forms of Greek. Pagan words like 'fullness', 'knowledge' and 'wisdom' still contain something of their original flavour, but they are also given new content to fit the good news of Jesus Christ. While the apostolic message is clearly influenced by its Greek context, yet it bends that context to fit it into God's revelation in Jesus Christ. Listening and learning does not necessarily require unbiblical compromise.

It should also be said that preaching for conversion need not preclude such listening and learning as befits true dialogue. Ajith Fernando, the Sri Lankan author of *Jesus and the World Religions*, has noted four objections to preaching Christ with the aim that people turn to him for new life and salvation. People claim that such proclamation is 'too narrow, ignoring the working of God in the other religions . . .', that it betrays an intolerant attitude of exclusiveness, is arrogant and that it reflects 'the imperialistic attitude of the colonial rulers'. Actually all Christians are called to rejoice in all that is good and true in other faiths, although we may grieve at the corrupting presence, too, of sin and untruth. Every Christian should also repent of every vestige of intolerance, arrogance or aggressive imperialism. Such characteristics of pride need not underlie a convinced and definite preaching of the good news of Jesus Christ.

2. Proclamation

Frank Whaling (*Christian Theology and World Religions*) comments that there are eight 'observable elements that are present within every religious tradition'. All faiths have a religious community, ritual, social involvement, ethics, scripture and myth, doctrinal concepts, artistic aesthetics and spirituality. While it is certainly true that all faiths have certain things in common, he rightly points out that they also disagree within the framework of these eight categories. As Christians we shall therefore rejoice when we see goodness, truth and beauty in other faiths. We are happy to agree on such matters. But this does not mean that we do not want to bring to all people the glorious reality and truth of Jesus Christ. Preaching remains central to our calling.

a) By life

In the Old Testament, Israel was not sent out to preach the glory of her God to the Gentiles. Rather she was called to live as God's people in obedience to his Law, so reflecting the beauty of God's own nature. The intention was that the Gentiles would *see* the glory of Israel's God in her communal life and in the personal lives of her people.

In the New Testament, too, Jesus' followers are called to show forth the nature of God's kingdom and its characteristics of righteousness, justice, peace and joy. Their love would shine like a beacon in a dark world, drawing people of all nations to believe in the Lord, love and worship him. Paul describes Christians as 'living epistles' written by Christ 'not with ink but with the Spirit of the living God' (2 Cor. 3:2–3). While we may not agree with Christopher Columbus in all things, he was surely right in his diaries to glory in his name 'Christopher', the one who bears Christ. He sensed the biblical truth that Christians are indwelt by the Spirit of Christ and so carry Christ within. Wherever the Christian goes, there Jesus Christ is also. It is a humbling thought, for we know that often our lives do not demonstrate the nature of Christ adequately. In our sin we present by our lives a distorted image of our Lord.

This distortion may be particularly marked when we are living in a cross-cultural situation, which is often the case when we are relating to people of other faiths. We know that everything we do tells a story. The way we walk speaks; the way we dress, shake hands, eat and drink – all say something of our character and our attitude to other people. But in different cultures we shall often be surprised at what we have unwittingly conveyed.

Some years ago when we lived in Indonesia we overheard some men describing the national characteristics of the English.

We suddenly realised that we ourselves were the only English people in that whole area, the only models of English people they could possibly have been observed. They were judging the English by our lives. It might not be wise at this stage to reveal what they said! It came home to us that people were not only judging the English by our lives, but also their view of Jesus Christ would be determined by the lives of his followers. That is much more serious!

b) By signs

We not only preach the good news of Jesus by our lives, but also by visible signs. In the Bible the word of God is often accompanied by such outward evidences of God's working. The rainbow supports God's promise to Noah; circumcision reminds Jewish men of God's covenant and their relationship to him; the pillar of cloud and fire demonstrated to the people of Israel that God was their king; the shaking of the temple foundations brought the proud prophet Isaiah to realise his sin; the miracles of Jesus and the apostles backed up their preached word; the physical elements of the Passover, the Lord's Supper and baptism have a message alongside the spoken word. We could multiply examples in Scripture of how sign and word go hand in hand. This is seen with particular clarity in John's Gospel where sign and word alternate to form together the full message of Jesus Christ.

God is so gracious in giving us visible evidence of the truth of his word to bolster our weak faith. When I first came to a living faith in Christ, God wonderfully answered even some rather stupid prayers in order to underline to me his reality and his grace. Many today are finding that God is confirming or renewing their faith through miraculous healings, the gift of tongues or other clear evidences that he is a God who is alive and who works. So for example the mushrooming Pentecostal Churches of South America expect miraculous healings to accompany their preaching of the gospel so that word and sign together will convince people of the truth in Jesus Christ.

c) By word

We must not separate the witness of our lives from the witness of our mouths. If we preach the good news, but our lives are a mess, then people will quickly note our hypocritical inconsistency. On the other hand, what will result from our living very attractive lives without any verbal witness? People will just praise us, 'What a lovely person he/she is!' So the glory will go to us rather than to the Lord.

We have already observed that in the Old Testament, Israel was called to witness to the Gentile nations around her only through her life. The one exception to this general rule is Jonah who was sent to preach to Nineveh. Through the message of the Book of Jonah, Israel was already being prepared for the later calling to go out to all nations to preach the word of God. In the New Testament however the followers of Jesus Christ are 'sent out to preach' (Mark 3:14). The out-going centrifugal mission of the New Testament is added to the in-gathering centripetal mission through the life of Israel. After the death and resurrection of Jesus, the coming of the Holy Spirit to the apostles drove them out into the world to proclaim the gospel. Jesus' gracious command, 'as the Father has sent me, even so I send you' (John 20:21), goes together with his breathing on them and saying 'receive the Holy Spirit'. So also in the Acts of the Apostles 1:8 the power of the Holy Spirit is linked to being 'my witnesses . . . to the end of the earth'. Indeed the Acts of the Apostles could equally well be called 'the Acts of the Holy Spirit' or 'the Book of Evangelistic Mission'. It is the Holy Spirit who sends the Church out into all peoples to preach the good news of Jesus and his resurrection.

Christian witness must be built on the foundation of holy and loving Christian lives, both individually and corporately in the fellowship of the Church. Human weakness often requires visible evidence of the reality and truth of God's goodness, so signs may be needed. But God consistently uses words as his primary means of communicating to his people and of revealing himself. It was by his word that he created the world – God's word really is powerful! And it is by his incarnate word, Jesus Christ, that he recreates, regenerates and reveals. So we are not surprised to find that Jesus' followers are called to go into all the world to preach a word that will reveal the Father through the Son by the Spirit. The mission of the Church must include verbal proclamation of the gospel.

Of course our witness of life and word must follow the pattern of our master, Jesus. His principal title is 'the suffering servant'. We too must walk in his footsteps of suffering and humble serving. We may well have to suffer severe criticism even from fellow Christians for our belief that Jesus is the one and only way to the Father, that people need to be born again as God's children through faith in Jesus Christ, his death and resurrection. In some countries even discreet and wise Christian witness may lead to imprisonment or worse. This may be particularly true in Muslim and Marxist nations. In other situations the suffering may be more subtle; we can be ridiculed, ostracised or discriminated against in promotion prospects. But the Christian is called to take up the cross and follow Jesus. We are also required to become servants like him. Sadly the very words 'the Lord's servant', 'Christian service' or 'the ministry' have been contaminated by the world's spirit of pride. They have become status words. So one minister once said to me that his congregation had an inadequate sense of 'the dignity of the ministry'! What dignity is there in being a slave? In coming to serve the world Jesus laid aside his glory, took the form of a slave and went right to the cross for our salvation (Phil. 2:5–8). Paul starts some of his epistles with the words 'I, Paul, a slave of Jesus Christ' (e.g. Rom. 1:1). We too in the witness of our lives and words should be humble slaves for Jesus' sake and for the sake of a lost world.

It is sometimes said that proclamation means pride. Such critics deny any faith in the absolute truth of God's self-revelation in his incarnate and his written word. It is true that some of us preach the Gospel with pride and lack of empathetic understanding of the other person. It is equally true that some critics of conversion preaching can be proud of their tolerance and of their broad sympathies.

But in the New Testament, Paul does boast! Not in his own gifts or abilities, but in the faith of other believers (2 Cor. 9:2) and particularly in the cross of Jesus Christ (Gal. 6:14). Perhaps Paul was also thinking of the Psalmist's declaration 'my soul makes its boast in the Lord' (Ps. 34:2). Let us indeed be beautifully and unashamedly proud of our Lord and of other believers in Christ, our brothers and sisters.

Conclusion

Because the quality of our lives and faith as Christians falls far short of God's perfect standards as revealed in his word, we have much to learn from the followers of other faiths. We recognise that they have in their traditions elements of truth, goodness and beauty despite the work of Satan and the corrupting evil which is all-pervasive. We need to be corrected by and to learn from people of every religious background. This is not only in order that we may be relevant in our witness to the Gospel of Jesus Christ, but also for our own sakes that we may grow towards the fullness of God's perfect self-revelation in Jesus Christ.

So we want to underline the benefits of listening and learning in non-monologue dialogue. But such discussion and debate should never preclude the longing to share with others what God has given to us in Jesus Christ. The former Bishop of Winchester, John Taylor, has said, 'We must covet for all men what, in our moments of highest aspiration, we covet for ourselves: the privilege of walking consciously in the steps and in the power of the Crucified . . . the fullness of life cannot mean less than that.' True dialogue will include the specific aim to persuade others to follow Jesus Christ, to accept his death and resurrection for our salvation. Dialogue and preaching represent the two sides of a single coin.

10

The Challenge of a
Multi-Faith World

Throughout this book we have maintained the Christian view that all faiths contain a remnant image of God with truth, goodness and beauty. Yet with sadness we have also noted that this truth and goodness betrays demonic corruption with the all-pervasive presence of sin and untruth. What then does this mean in terms of our practical approach to relationships with those of other faiths? In our contemporary world of religious pluralism we cannot allow this subject to remain in the stratosphere of mere theory, but must bring it down to earth in the realities of day-to-day issues.

1. Internationally

Assuming as they do that religion has little significance in the real world, Western media and secular NGOs sometimes ignore the role of religious convictions in shaping the movements of world politics. I remember the days of American protests against involvement in the Vietnam War. While glaring car headlights witnessed to their drivers' opposition to American participation in this far-off Asian struggle, magazines and newspapers bulged with lengthy articles about Vietnam, Cambodia and Laos. To my surprise not one article seemed to note the religious differences between Laos, Cambodia and Vietnam. Writers assumed that Laos and Cambodia would naturally relate well to Vietnam, failing to observe that the culture and faith of Mahayana Buddhism may not cohabit with Theravada Buddhists. Since then history has demonstrated the impossibility of Vietnam's former attempt to unite Laos and Cambodia with herself.

Britain lost out in Iran in the early days of Khomeini's Shi'ite revolution against the Shah. The British authorities backed the wrong horse because they assumed that the economic and military power of the Shah would hold the trump card over fanatical religious enthusiasm. Since then we have begun to learn the power of religious conviction to move the multitudes, topple governments and motivate destructive wars like that between Iran and Iraq. And more recent acts of terrorism in the USA and elsewhere have been inspired by the principle of Jihad in Islam.

Religious and cultural disunity has threatened to tear the very heart out of Northern Ireland and turned idyllic and prosperous Lebanon into a horrific battlefield wilderness. Fighting between extremist Muslim movements in Afghanistan was followed by destructive warfare against the Muslim Taliban. seventy thousand slit throats in Algeria have turned the masses of that nation against more fundamentalist Islam. Hindu–Muslim tensions have caused the deaths of thousands in India, while Sikhs battle for independence from Hindu India and shake the very foundations of Indian democracy. To India's south the island of Sri Lanka suffers from the bitter opposition of its Hindu Tamils to the rule of Buddhist Singhalese. And such divisions along religious lines may be found not only in Asia. In Africa, too, Roman Catholics and Protestants struggle against each other in Lesotho, Muslims fight against Christians in Nigeria, Sudan, Egypt and other countries.

In our global village, world religious communities have got to learn to live together in tolerant peace. Even if they disagree theologically and long to see other people converted to their faith, loving tolerance and peaceful co-existence remain essential for the welfare of our planet. Despite A. Toynbee's assumption that the 'plague of exclusivity' always produces 'dogmatic intolerance' and H. Kung's clever statement that 'absolute truth becomes tolerant only when people no longer believe in it', full assurance of absolute truth in God's revelation need not be accompanied by arrogant intolerance. Indeed it may well lead to humble gratitude for God's gift of grace and a loving desire that others should in God's time enter into the life and truth found in God's word. As we have already noted, so-called tolerant people may actually be more intolerant than those of exclusivist theology. They may only be tolerant of those who share their own liberal outlook. It is true that people with a sure faith can sometimes be equally intolerant, but they may also respect convinced believers of other faiths. Biblical Christians will long for the conversion of other people and will therefore share the gospel with them, but we believe that conversion is entirely the work of the Holy Spirit. We can only patiently, humbly and lovingly bear witness and pray.

2. Racialism

We have just seen that often religion and culture go hand in hand. It may also be true that religious communities are divided along ethnic lines. So in Britain, Islam is centred largely on Pakistani and Bengali communities, while those peoples view Christianity as the white British faith. It is easy to harden lines of division through inaccurate stereotypes – 'Christianity is white', 'Islam is Arab and Asian'. In such circumstances it is only too easy for religious disagreements to take on racialist overtones and vice versa. Evangelistic witness can be seen as racialist aggression. We have seen this in the violent reactions of the

Jewish Chronicle against even the most gentle practice of evangelism among Jews in Britain. It is seen as anti-Semitic and thus racialist.

British society has allowed racial prejudice to become common. People from ethnic minorities are discriminated against in the labour market, finding it almost impossible to break into many forms of work. If one white person and one black person apply for a vacancy and have similar qualifications, it is generally unlikely that the black person will be given the job. Discrimination in housing and violence on the streets cause untold hardship and bitterness to many in the ethnic minority communities. It is vitally important that Christians should stand out against all discrimination, for the biblical message underlines the enormous importance of justice in the eyes of a holy God. In the Bible, personal righteousness is inseparably linked to social justice. Together with the command to love God come the equally vital words that we should love our neighbour. And the Gospels make it clear that our neighbour may not be of the same racial background. It was a Samaritan who helped the Jew in need.

So the Christian Church is required to play an active role in opposition to all forms of racialism within our society. Likewise we are called to demonstrate in the life of the Church that racial divisions have been broken down by the uniting love of Jesus Christ. Jew and Gentile, black and white, become brothers and sisters in the Church family, for in Christ we have all equally become God's children. Later in this chapter we shall look at the question of churches consisting of one race or culture alone, but at this stage let us affirm that the Christian faith demands that we demonstrate practically our loving unity across all racial, cultural or class barriers. With penitence we have to confess that our Churches have often failed to live up to their calling, allowing racialist prejudices to persist in our midst.

Our failure to take the lead in opposition to racialism within our society has meant that other non-Christians have gained the initiative in this battle. Now we are frequently faced with the difficult question of whether to join forces with extreme left-wing groups who organise demonstrations or other action against racialism. Of course Christians delight to work together with any group in the pursuit of righteousness or justice. But while such people campaign for racial equality, they often include hidden agendas which favour the practice of homosexuality, abortion or other issues with which Christians may not be in agreement. It is not always easy therefore to know when to side with other groups in denouncing discrimination.

3. Religious Education

In our pluralist society educational authorities have seen the importance that children be taught about the various religions found within our country.

But how should children be taught about the religions? Debate rages on whether to concentrate on giving pupils a feel of the forms of worship and devotion practised by each religion. Others have stressed the importance of children understanding the doctrinal beliefs of the various faiths. Yet others have wanted to stress the fundamental oneness of all religions, so minimising the differences between them. This has sometimes led to all the religions being reduced to their lowest common denominator. More recently objections have been raised against this approach, for it implies that all religion is somewhat insipid.

If we teach a little about all the major faiths, we may end up with insufficient time in the curriculum to give adequate attention to any of them. Is it then right to concentrate on a proper teaching of the Christian faith because it is the historic tradition of this country? It is certainly true that Christianity has played a vital part in forming the culture and thought forms of our community. But then we have to ask whether it is right to impose Christian teaching on children from homes which follow other faiths. Should Islam become the main religion to be taught in some of our city schools where the majority of the children are of Muslim extraction?

In Northern Ireland religious prejudices have been continued through separated education. Roman Catholic schools have catered for the children of the minority community, thus leaving the state schools almost exclusively to Protestant youngsters. In this way religious education has also followed sectarian lines, but one has to ask whether this has actually benefited society overall. This situation may stand as a warning against having segregated schools along racial or religious lines. Indeed we have to ask whether it is wise to allow different streams of religious education for the various faith communities – Islam for the Muslims, Sikhism for the Sikhs, Christianity for Christians, etc. And yet all research shows that faith schools attain considerably better results both in academic success and in moral character formation. Liberal secular schools in general fall far short.

School assemblies present us with a further thorny question. It must be right to have the whole school together for these in order to foster a sense of school identity. In the past most school assemblies had a definite religious content with Bible reading, hymn singing and prayer in the name of Christ. Can this be imposed on non-Christian children? If not, should we abandon all religious content and turn assemblies into purely secular occasions? Or should we again fall into the lowest common denominator syndrome and only have Scripture readings, hymns and prayers which offend nobody? But then none of the religions will acknowledge such religious practice as in any way worthy. One solution in a really multi-racial school would be to encourage each religion to take turns in holding a full-blooded worship time according to their own practice, but warn other children that there may be parts of it in which in good conscience they cannot participate. But at least the worship would always be genuine and all children would observe how others worship. But even this solution presents us with major problems. Muslims, Christians and Jews might feel that some religions' worship actually does involve demonic activity and they might not be willing therefore even to be present.

The climate of opinion in Europe has discouraged assured religious conviction. It has become unacceptable for Christian teachers to teach about their faith in such a way that expresses their own conviction. Christian teachers have sometimes felt therefore that they are pushed into a position where they have to compromise their faith. One wonders whether it might not be more honest and more attractive if teachers shared openly why they hold the particular religious convictions that they have. Of course it would not be right to pressurise children to be converted to the teacher's beliefs, but that is true not only for teachers but also in all other situations. In no situation is it ethical to place undue pressure on another person to convert to our faith or likewise to their agnostic liberalism. And as a Christian such pressure would demonstrate an inadequate faith in the work of the Holy Spirit, who alone can bring people to new birth in Christ.

4. Multi-Faith Worship

Related to the above debates is the whole question of multi-faith worship or prayer services. Convinced Christians may be invited to such events, but question whether it involves spiritual compromise. It seems to me that the Christian always has to ask what attendance at such activities actually says to other people. As Christians we need to remember that Jesus Christ taught that he is the truth. In following Jesus we must therefore hold firmly to truth. Nothing we do or say should convey untruth. If our attendance at a multi-faith service gives the impression that we accept all religions as equally valid, then we have to absent ourselves from it. If on the other hand our attendance merely tells people that we want good relationships in society, then perhaps it is acceptable. But still we have to remember that we shall again and again be faced with the embarrassing situation that many of the constituent parts of the service may be against our beliefs. We shall then need to refrain from participation in that particular prayer or song. It is quite possible that such selective participation may prove more offensive than actually staying right away from the service. Then we have also to face honestly the possibility of demonic activity in all forms of worship which deny Jesus Christ and concentrate on deities which have removed him from the glory and honour which we believe to be his due.

As individuals many of us have rejoiced in the opportunity to share in prayer with people of other faiths, but without compromising our Christian beliefs. In such situations it is important that both the Christian and the other person should know what the other believes and should not be given the impression that we underestimate the importance of our particular beliefs. We should also make it clear that we do not believe that all religions have equal validity. But particularly with Jews and Muslims we can have the confidence that we pray to the same God even if our theological understanding of some aspects of his nature and work may differ.

5. Good Neighbours

Different cultures can sometimes find it hard to understand each other and live closely together. Different foods not only taste strange to others, but may also produce smells which other races' noses may not enjoy. The way we run our families and homes may vary from one ethnic community to another. This can also cause misunderstanding. Each group has its own idea of what forms the basis of good manners. It may therefore take considerable mutual patience and tolerance if we are to break through to truly deep relationships of love and trust with neighbours of other races. In doing so both sides will have to lay aside all sorts of racial prejudices not only in themselves, but also in other people around them.

Cross-cultural and inter-religious friendships take time to develop. We have to win each other's confidence step by step. It requires gentle patience. Such friendships may start at the level of very practical help in little things. Some within ethnic minority communities are finding it hard to learn the English language well and appreciate help in this. Others may be baffled by the complicated intricacies of form filling and other social red tape. Many parents are struggling to understand issues facing their young people who are being educated in British schools and are making friends with children from other communities. And this problem becomes critical if such friendships develop into serious relationships between teenage boys and girls. Some children of Sikh, Muslim or Hindu parents are beginning to lose their faith under the religiously liberal influence of Western education. This can cause tremendous heartache to their parents. Many Christian parents will understand this agony only too well and it may prove mutually encouraging to share that together. This will almost inevitably involve both sets of parents sharing together what their faith really means to them and will lead in an unthreatening way to genuine witness.

When deep inter-religious friendships are forged, then it becomes much easier and more natural to share one's faith. Such witness cannot be attacked with the pejorative label of 'proselytising', nor can it be said that it makes use of immoral means or undue pressure. In all real friendships we should share together what is of primary significance in our lives, namely our faith. And as Christians we shall naturally make it clear that we earnestly desire that our friends would come to enjoy the fullness of life in Christ together with us. We believe that those who believe in Jesus Christ have new life now in this world and eternal life in the hereafter. We shall not put any wrong pressure on our friends to accept Jesus as their Lord and Saviour, but we have a right and a responsibility lovingly to share that with them.

Some friendships will lead to genuine conversions, some will not. That is ultimately the responsibility of the Holy Spirit. But we do not engage in such friendships only in order to witness, so our relationship with our neighbours will not depend on how they respond to our faith. We are called to love our neighbours for their own sake, not just as potential Christians.

6. Be Yourself

Genuine relationships demand an open-hearted honesty in which neither person masks the truth. We need not only to be truthful about ourselves and the cultural backgrounds which so influence us, but also about the realities of our faith. In relating to those of other faiths it is a great temptation to try to conceal our weaknesses and difficulties lest we discourage our friend from being convinced of the truth. We so easily fall into the trap of recounting all the wonderful things people of our faith have done throughout history. Christians love to remember how the evangelical revival led on to the freedom of slaves through Wilberforce and Buxton as well as social reform through Shaftesbury and others. Early missionaries throughout the world pioneered medical care, education and many social reforms. Of course there is truth in these facts and some modern critics of the Christian faith should give credit where it is due. But these positive outworkings of the Christian gospel have to be put alongside failures. Christians have sometimes supported injustice and oppression. Some were involved in the genocide of the holocaust under Hitler. And such movements in history as the Crusades leave a bitter taste in the memories of Muslims and Jews.

In our theology, too, we need to be honest that our rejoicing in the glory of Jesus Christ and the gospel does not preclude serious debates within Christian circles. For example, the doctrine of the Trinity is the source of our assurance that God not only remains in the unknowable splendour of absolute holiness, but also stoops down to live incarnate among us as Immanuel, God with us. But the satisfying truth of the Trinity still leaves us with immense theological difficulties to which we can find no easy solutions. Likewise we have to admit that the divine-humanity of Jesus not only excites us, but also presents us with problems. And all of us tend in practice to underplay his divinity or his humanity in the daily realities of our Christian experience. Equally our doctrine of biblical revelation proves wonderfully applicable to the questions of the modern world, but it also leaves us with major theological battles on our hands. God has revealed his word by the inspiration of the Holy Spirit, but through human beings. It is marked by the imprint of the historical and cultural background of the writers, but equally its absolute reliability is guaranteed by its God-given inspiration. This allows the flexibility of cultural adaptability in differing eras of history or in the various countries where the Scriptures are read, but Christians do not find it easy to hold the divine inspiration and the human authorship together.

So we need to be honest with our friends not only about what we consider to be the positive aspects of our faith, but also to share truthfully what difficulties we experience. This is true not only of our beliefs, but also of our spiritual life. Let us be honest about what we experience concerning prayer, temptation, or doubt. Only then can we honestly expect others to be open with us.

7. The Church

The reality of our Christian faith is experienced within the life of the Church. Again it is important that we should be open both about the tremendous privileges we have in being part of God's Church, but also about some of the weaknesses and failures of the Church.

In thinking about the Christian approach to those of other faiths, it is vital that we consider the corporate nature of the Church. The credal definition of the nature of the Church is as 'one Holy, Catholic and Apostolic Church'.

a) One

While it is true that Christians need to repent with deep humility of our disunity and lack of love both in our congregations and also between churches, still we rejoice in the measure of family love we enjoy together as brothers and sisters in Christ, children of our heavenly Father. Again we need to be honest about our failures when talking with people of other faiths – and they will share the sense of grief and penitence we have, for their faiths too know the tragedy of disunity. All the world's religions experience the bitter sin of lack of love and even fighting between different groupings.

But as Christians we are not called to remain for ever in the heartbreak of repentance, but to know the cleansing forgiveness of Christ and the joy of new life. It is therefore our privilege to experience some measure of the love of Christ within his Church. The apostle John pointed out in his first letter (1 John 3:14) that our love for our brothers and sisters is a sure mark that we have passed from death to life. John even declares that if we do not love our brother/sister, we cannot be children of God (1 John 3:10). The converse is equally true. As God's children we inherit his nature of love and his Spirit produces within us the fruit of the Spirit, the first of which is love (Gal. 3:22). Although our love remains imperfect and still needs to develop and grow, yet nevertheless God's love is evident within the family of his Church.

As one who travels quite widely, I find this family love something very special. Wherever one goes, brothers and sisters immediately receive you in love and there is immediately a deep bond. The love of Christ overrides all denominational or national boundaries, binding us together in loving unity whatever our background.

It is vitally important that we demonstrate the love of Christ before the eyes of our friends of other religious backgrounds. They should be drawn towards the Lord because they see our love for each other in the Church and also our love for all people. A warm Christian fellowship will attract men and women to our Lord.

b) Holy

The constant biblical emphasis on God's holiness needs to be embodied in the life of the Church. Muslims particularly point the finger at any moral failures among Christians, stressing their own ethics of purity. Christians will have no real witness unless they demonstrate a godly righteousness and dissociate themselves from some of the less desirable aspects of Western life. Muslims may assume that drunkenness, sexual immorality and Dallas-style materialism reflect Christianity in action. So in Tunisia a taxi driver told me that tourists' drunkenness and topless bathing were of course Christian. He was surprised when as a Christian I separated myself from these things.

Christian righteousness should be seen in social questions as well as in private morality. In our modern world it is a vital part of our testimony that we stand against all oppression and injustice in favour of true relationships of equal rights and mutual respect. Social or political aggression cannot be tolerated by Christians and we must take a lead in opposing them.

It is also true that our evangelistic patterns should reflect the love and gracious holiness which we profess. Rightly used, the word 'proselytise' implies forms of evangelism which use undue moral pressure or even financial bribery. Sadly this word is sometimes used to denigrate all evangelism of whatever form. With the model of Christ and the apostles in mind, we would reject all proselytisation, but maintain the right and responsibility to share the gospel in truth, love and humility. But truth, love and humility do not negate our longing that all people should turn in repentance and faith to Jesus Christ as the way to God the Father. Our evangelism will not be aggressive or unrighteous, but it will be humbly confident.

c) Catholic

Since the call of Abraham in Genesis 12, God's purposes for all peoples has been through his chosen people Israel, but with the advent of the Messiah, Jesus, God has reached out to the wider world of the Samaritans and the Gentiles of all nations. No longer do the Gentiles have to join themselves as proselytes to Israel, but they can follow the Messiah and yet still remain entirely within their own culture.

Over the past centuries the Gospel of Jesus Christ has spread widely through the continents. No longer can it be said that Christianity is a North Atlantic phenomenon. Large Jewish–Christian fellowships have been born in America, Israel and elsewhere to remind us of the Church's origins. Latin American, African and Asian Churches abound with spiritual energy and growth, often outdoing their equivalent Churches in the Western world.

This has led to the thorny question of national Churches whose character reflects the cultural forms of the host people. Christians sometimes disagree how far this may be allowable. Is it right for Jewish fellowships to shrug off long centuries of Gentile patterns of Church structures and worship? What in Jewish traditional culture can be introduced into Christian congregations without compromising biblical truth? The debate may be even more strongly contested when it relates to Muslim, Hindu or Buddhist backgrounds. If Messianic synagogues offend some Gentile Christians, the very thought of Messianic mosques or temples will send shivers of apprehension down some Christian spines. Of course all Christians have constantly to ask themselves whether in adjusting to their particular societies they may not be compromising in some way. This applies to Western Christians too. The fundamental question facing us is, 'Is the Lord Jesus Christ central in our faith and practice and are we obedient to the word of God in Scripture?' Then in answering this we remind ourselves that in the Bible the universality of the Church of God has a central place. In our relationship with those of other faiths it is vital that we reflect in our fellowships the international character of God's Church.

Because of our belief that all religions and cultures consist of a mixture of truth and error, we recognise that the Christian Church will happily continue some aspects of those cultures while at the same time renouncing anything which is not consonant with the lordship of Christ and the revealed truths of God's word. In relationship to cultures from which the Church emerges there will always be both continuity and discontinuity. Too much emphasis on continuity will lead to syncretistic compromise, while undue stress on discontinuity will result in the Church becoming a culturally alien ghetto of irrelevance.

d) Apostolic

From the outset of Church history, as seen in the book of the Acts of the Apostles, the Church was sent out by the Holy Spirit to preach the Gospel of Jesus Christ. Indeed this out-going commission began in the Gospels with the original call of the twelve disciples (Mark 3:14) who were not only called to be with the Lord, but also to 'be sent out to preach'. This original call was reinforced at the end of the incarnate life of Jesus when he commanded his disciples to 'go and make disciples of all nations' (Matt. 28:19). Each person of the Trinity is involved in sending the Church out to preach to all peoples. The Father sends his Son, who in turn sends his disciples (John 20:21). This verse is immediately followed by Jesus breathing on them with the gift of the Holy Spirit (John 20:22), an obvious prelude to the full empowering by the Holy Spirit at Pentecost (Acts 1:8) which drives the apostles out as witnesses 'to the end of the earth'.

The Church loses one fundamental aspect of its very identity if it fails to allow itself to be sent out to preach the Gospel of Jesus Christ. Again and again in this book I have sought to underline the importance of wisdom, humility and love in our witness, but these characteristics should never negate our call to preach the good news of Jesus Christ with the clear aim that men and women of all races and backgrounds might come to life-giving faith in him and be joined to his Church.

8. The Kingdom

The worldwide, apostolic mission is linked to the kingdom of heaven and the kingship of Christ. This was not accidental, for the task of Christian mission cannot be separated from the biblical concept of God's kingdom. So it was with John the Baptist and Jesus himself. Their mission began with the declaration, 'Repent, for the kingdom of heaven is at hand' (Matt. 3:2 and 4:17). So it is good for us to define our mission-calling in terms of the kingdom of heaven.

Traditional Jewish thought has attributed certain specific characteristics to the kingdom of heaven. The apostle Paul defines these as 'righteousness and peace and joy in the Holy Spirit', adding that those who thus serve Christ are acceptable to God (Rom. 14:17–18). These descriptive characteristics must have been in the back of John's and Jesus' minds as they declared that the kingdom was at hand.

a) Righteousness

The absolute purity of God's holy righteousness determines the nature of his divine kingdom. The kingdom and righteousness cannot be separated. Where God's kingdom rules, there right-eousness must be seen. No righteousness means no kingdom.

Jewish thought has believed that the kingdom of heaven would come to pass when Israel demonstrated righteousness by keeping the whole Law for even one day. Thus it was thought that the righteousness of God's people would precede the coming of the kingdom. Righteousness was seen as the necessary condition for the ushering in of God's reign.

Jesus turns this teaching on its head. He too associates the coming of the kingdom with an accompanying righteousness, but he announces that the kingdom would come first. Then God's rule would necessitate a new righteousness in his people. Because the kingdom of heaven was at hand, he called the people to repentance. The presence of the kingdom would not tolerate a careless continuing in sin. While it is true that Jesus, the king of the kingdom, comes to sinners rather than to the righteous, he nevertheless demands such repentance as will lead to a new life of righteousness.

Paul adds a further insight into this truth. He sees that the sacrificial death of Jesus justifies sinners who believe in Jesus Christ. By God's grace we are considered to be righteous because our sin is covered by the righteousness of Christ. So in the kingdom of God the believer in Christ is reckoned righteous and then gradually made righteous by the work of the indwelling Holy Spirit.

The task of mission is to introduce people to God's kingdom and pray that they might enter into that kingdom by faith in Jesus Christ. The Church must demonstrate in her communal and individual living the reality of kingdom righteousness, so that people can see the kingdom lived out before their eyes. Such a demonstration of righteousness should form the basis for the work of the Holy Spirit in convicting people of their sinfulness and their need of the saving work of Jesus Christ. Then it is also the task of the Church to proclaim the good news of Jesus' death and resurrection, God's means of salvation.

In the Old Testament righteousness is closely tied to the idea of justice. Justice and righteousness are two sides of the same coin. For simplicity's sake we may say that while righteousness denotes personal holiness, justice stands for social holiness. The kingdom of heaven requires not only personal morality, but also a new holiness in social relationships. These social relationships are within the family, in our work places, in our local neighbourhood and more widely in our whole nation and worldwide. Socio-political issues lie at the very heart of kingdom life therefore.

The kingdom demands that we be lovingly concerned and active for justice in all areas of society both in our national life and also internationally.

While the Old Testament so frequently links righteousness with justice, there is a strange lack of the word 'justice' in the New Testament. The two Hebrew words in the Old Testament seem to give way to just one Greek word for righteousness in the New Testament. In the New Testament however another word comes to the fore – fellowship or *koinonia*. The concept of justice in fact implies that we belong together as one united people. Fellowship likewise means that we relate to each other in love and sharing. Neither in justice nor in fellowship can there be any idea of oppression, selfishness or proud denigration of others. In fact the New Testament follows the pattern of the Old Testament in stressing God's loving concern for the poor and oppressed, the widow and the orphan, the stranger in your land.

In the Old Testament both righteousness and justice were to be practised within Israel as the people of God, but always with the aim that the nations should see, be attracted and thus come to worship the God of Israel. In the New Testament, too, the Church as the redeemed people of God is called to demonstrate righteousness and justice to the world with the aim that people might turn from their sin and believe in the king of the kingdom, Jesus himself. It is also the task of the Church to teach the world about true moral righteousness and social justice with relation-ships of fellowship. We are to work in the world to bring about these characteristics of the kingdom as far as possible, but we do realise that all humankind needs the power of Christ's Holy Spirit to enable us to put these kingdom characteristics into practice. We all also need the atoning work of Christ to cleanse us of our sin, for all of us fall far short of God's standards in these matters.

In the Old Testament we observe Israel's long history of failure. The surrounding nations were not presented with an ideal model of kingdom life. This is also sadly true of the history of the Christian Church. The life of the Church is not always characterised by holiness of living, nor do we observe that oneness and love which fellowship implies. Quarrelling and disunity represent serious denials of the kingdom – we notice how serious a matter it was to Paul when two Christian women quarrelled (Phil. 4:2) and this situation may well have formed the background to his great teaching on the person of Christ in Philippians 2:1–11. So the presence of God's kingdom in our midst moves us to repentance.

b) Peace

The second of Paul's characteristics of the kingdom is contained in the much-loved Hebrew word, shalom. The prophet Isaiah also joins peace to righteousness and justice as marks of the kingdom of Immanuel, the Lord God who is with us (Isa. 9:6–7). The word 'shalom' conveys an atmosphere which is beautiful, but it is hard to define exactly. As an everyday word of greeting, shalom conveys a sense of well-being and inner harmony. It is based on the fact that our sin has been covered (Ps. 32:1; Rom. 4:7–8) and therefore we can have a relationship of peace with God (Rom. 5:1). But this peace with God is not some irrelevant pietistic affair, for it influences every side of our lives and all our relationships within society. It also produces an inner peacefulness which dispels turbulent tensions, opens the door to happy interaction with others and allows us to engage in social issues without having some personal axe to grind. As John makes clear in his account of Jesus' resurrection, peace is an antidote to fear when the world is against us. He tells how the disciples were huddled together in fear with the doors carefully shut, but then the resurrected Jesus 'came and stood among them' (John 20:19,26) and greeted them with the significant 'shalom', 'Peace be with you' (John 20:19,21,26).

As also with righteousness and justice we are very aware that the Church has not yet entered into the fullness of its inheritance in the kingdom. We still have a long way to go and we look forward to the final perfection of the kingdom when we shall know the fullness of righteousness, justice and peace. Until the kingdom has come, we still need to pray 'Thy kingdom come.' Nevertheless it is our task in the world to demonstrate the reality of peace in our personal lives and in the communal life of the Church as the people of God. We are also called to work for peace even beyond the borders of the Church, for we know that the kingdom of God extends beyond the confines of the Church. The kingdom is not co-extensive with the Church. But we are called too to preach the good news of Jesus to all humankind, for people cannot recognise the gracious rule of God without being born again into his kingdom (John 3:3). Through faith in Jesus Christ we can enter the kingdom, becoming part of the Church worldwide which is the family of God. Then too we may grow in the experience and appreciation of God's gift of peace.

c) Joy in the Holy Spirit

The third characteristic of the kingdom of heaven is joy in the Holy Spirit (Rom. 14:17). It is significant that Paul links joy with the Holy Spirit, for the biblical idea of joy is not just ordinary human happiness. Rather it is a deep inner contentment which comes from the presence of Christ. Indeed in the Old Testament the so-called 'royal psalms' or 'kingship psalms' are marked by joy in the reality of worship. Worship of the living Lord brings true joy. Although it remains true that the kingdom of God is operative outside the confines of the Church, nevertheless the fullness of true joy cannot be separated from union with and worship of the Lord. While it is true therefore that Christian mission aims to bring into being conditions where people can be as happy as possible, still we need to be aware that evangelism is God's means through the Church of bringing people into faith in Christ and so into true joy in the Holy Spirit.

It is again important that the Church should not only preach the good news of a saviour in whose kingdom there is fullness of joy, but that we should also demonstrate joy in our personal lives and in our churches. It is a travesty of the truth if Christians are marked by long faces of misery. This does not mean that Christians are shielded from the tragedies and heartaches of this world, nor does it mean that we are to adopt glib smiles in the face of suffering. But the miraculous work of the Holy Spirit gives a deep sense of joy even in the midst of agonising suffering. So the letter to the Colossians speaks of a God-given power which leads to 'all endurance and patience with joy, giving thanks to the Father' (Col. 1:11–12). Some modern 'prosperity teaching' offers joy when we thrive. The ancient stoics taught patient endurance in the midst of suffering. The Holy Spirit alone can work the miracle in us which enables us to know the joy of the Lord and be thankful to God in times of suffering. What a relevant message of good news for today's suffering world!

This then is the task of mission for messengers of the kingdom. We are called as the people of God to demonstrate the true nature of God's rule in righteousness, justice, peace and joy. It is God's purpose that the life of the Church should attract people to our Lord so that they may join us in repentance, faith, worship and loving service. This call to live the life of the kingdom is matched by the New Testament command to the Church to proclaim the good news of Jesus Christ to all the world, inviting all people to turn from every form of idol, to believe in Jesus Christ as the one Saviour and Lord, and to join the family of God in the Church of Christ.

Jesus Christ did not have a purely heavenly nature, but identified with humanity as a Jew of the first century. It is therefore important that his disciples throughout all ages should also be identified with the historical contexts and cultures around them. Not only is the cross-cultural missionary called to adapt to the cultural forms and philosophy of the people among whom he or she works, but the local believers also need to relate to their own culture in the external forms and structures of the Church, in biblical interpretation and in theological expression. But it has also to be said that Jesus remained without sin when he identified with ordinary people of his time. So too the Church's contextualisation should not distort the Christian faith in ways that compromise the truth of the gospel. It is a matter of considerable debate how the gospel relates to culture and just how far contextualisation can go before it becomes heretical compromise, but the aim of cultural identification without syncretism is reasonably clear.

In discussing such complex issues as contextualisation it is vital that we do not lose sight of the central fact of the Christian faith – Jesus is Lord. This ancient credal confession must remain the heart of our faith and of our message to the world. And we as Christians need to come back to it in repentance again and again, for we so easily fail to practise what we preach. But it is significant that the New Testament message starts by stressing the kingdom of heaven; however, it continues by increasingly emphasising Jesus Christ, the king of the kingdom. Our aim in mission and in all our relationships with those of other faiths must be that ultimately Jesus may be pre-eminent (Col. 1:18).

Conclusion – The Goal

In discussing our relationship with those of other faiths we should not lose sight of our ultimate aim. Both in the Old Testament and in the New Testament the purpose of the life and work of God's people is that the name of the Lord should be honoured and glorified. The Christian will be saddened if the name of the Lord Jesus Christ is brought into disrepute, his glory denied and his work for us rejected. The goal of each individual Christian and of the Church as a body must be to witness to the glory of Father, Son and Holy Spirit in such ways that multitudes of men and women from every people might love and worship God.

This goal is described in the Bible in terms of people of every nation, tribe, people and tongue forming a great multitude 'before the throne and before the Lamb' (Rev. 7:9). The prophets Isaiah and Habakkuk foresaw the day when 'the earth will be filled with the knowledge of the glory of the Lord, as the waters cover the sea' (Hab. 2:14; Isa. 11:9). In our mission we earnestly desire and pray that the knowledge of God experienced in other faiths might be perfected through the full revelation of God in Christ and in the biblical scriptures. We long too that all sin and error might be redeemed and cleansed through faith in the atoning work of the Messianic Saviour, Jesus Christ. Then too in humility and repentance all of us confess our need of the indwelling Holy Spirit to sanctify us, make us increasingly holy and renew us after the image of God in which we were created (Col. 3:10).

The Bible makes it abundantly clear that the apostolic mission cannot be narrowed down to our own nation or people only. The Early Church had to learn that the kingdom of heaven should include all peoples, Jews as well as Gentiles, who followed their traditional religions. God longs that all might come to him in repentance and faith through his Messiah, Jesus Christ. We need to lift up our eyes today beyond the boundaries of our own people to bring the kingship of Christ to all peoples everywhere. We are called to worldwide mission.

Bibliography

G. Anderson and T. Stransky, *Christ's Lordship and Religious Pluralism*, Orbis 1981.

Sir Norman Anderson, *Christianity and World Religions*, IVP 1984.

B. Animananda, *The Blade: Life and Work of Brahmabandhab Upadhyaya*, Calcutta, Anvil 4/Z 1987.

W. Ariarajah, *Bible and People of Other Faiths*, WCC 1985.

G. Beasley-Murray, *Jesus and the Kingdom of God*, Eerdmans 1986.

J. Blauw, *The Missionary Nature of the Church*, Lutterworth 1962.

D. Bleich, *With Perfect Faith*, Hebrew Publications, New York 1980.

BMU, *Towards a Theology for Inter-Faith Dialogue*, BMU 1984.

D. Bosch, *Witness to the World*, Marshall, Morgan and Scott 1980.

British Council of Churches, *Relations with People of Other Faiths*, BCC 1981.

M. Buber, *I and Thou*, T. and T. Clark 1971.

M. Buber, *The Kingdom of God*. Published in German 1932, in English 1967. Horizon Press.

M. Buber, *Writings on the Principle of Dialogue*. Published in Dialogisches Leben 1947.

A. Camps, *Partners in Dialogue*, Orbis 1983.

H. Coward, *Pluralism, Challenge to World Religions*, Orbis 1985.

K. Cracknell, *Towards a New Relationship*, Epworth 1986.

K. Cracknell and Ç. Lamb, *Theology on Full Alert*, BCC 1984.

K. Cragg, *The Christ and the Faith*, SPCK 1986.

K. Cragg, *The Pen and the Faith*, George Allen & Unwin 1985.

K. Cragg, *Sandals at the Mosque*, SCM 1959.

A. Crollius, *The Word in the Experience of Revelation in Qur'an and Hindu Scriptures*, Universita Gregoriana, Rome 1974.

J. G. Davies, *Dialogue with the World*, SCM 1967.

G. D'Costa, *Christian Uniqueness Reconsidered*, Orbis 1990.

G. D'Costa, *John Hick's Theology of Religions*, University Press of America 1987.

G. D'Costa, *Theology and Religious Pluralism*, Blackwell 1986.

R. De Ridder, *Discipling the Nations*, Baker 1971.

V. Donovan, *Christianity Rediscovered*, SCM 1978.

J. Dupuis, *Toward a Christian Theology of Religious Pluralism*, Orbis 1997.

M. Eliade, *Patterns in Comparative Religion*, Sheed and Ward 1958.

A. Fernando, *I Believe in the Supremacy of Christ*, Hodder & Stoughton 1997.

A. Fernando, *Jesus and the World Religions*, Tyndale House 1987.

T. Fornberg, *The Problem of Christianity in Multi-Religious Societies Today*, Edwin Mellen Press 1995.

M. Goldsmith, *Good News for All Nations*, Hodder & Stroughton 2002.

M. Goldsmith, *Islam and Christian Witness*, MARC 1982.

M. Goldsmith, *Jesus and His Relationships*, Paternoster 2000.

M. Goldsmith, *Matthew and Mission: The Gospel Through Jewish Eyes*, Paternoster 2001.

M. Goldsmith and R. Harley, *Who is My Neighbour*, Scripture Union 1988.

G. Gutierrez, *A Theology of Liberation*, Orbis 1973.

D. M. Hay, *Exploring Inner Space*, Mowbray 1987.

S. M. Heim, *Is Christ the Only Way*, Judson Press 1985.

S. M. Heim, *Salvations: Truth and Difference in Religion*, Orbis 1995.

J. Hick, *Christianity and Other Religions*, Fortress Press 1987.

J. Hick, *God Has Many Names: Britain's New Religious Pluralism*, Macmillan 1980.

J. Hick, *The Myth of God Incarnate*, SCM 1977.

J. Hick, *The Rainbow of Faiths: Critical Dialogue and Religious Pluralism*, SCM 1995.

J. Hick, *Truth and Dialogue*, Sheldon Press 1974.

J. Hick and P. Knitter, *The Myth of Christian Uniqueness*, SCM 1988.

R. Hooker, *Outside the Camp*, CLS, Madras 1972.

R. Hooker and C. Lamb, *Love the Stranger*, SPCK 1986.

A. G. Hunter, *Christianity and other Faiths in Britain*, SCM 1985.

K. Kitamori, *Theology of the Pain of God*, SCM 1966.

K. Klostermaier, *Mythologies and Philosophies of Salvation in the Theistic Traditions of India*, Wilfrid Laurier University Press 1984.

P. F. Knitter, *No Other Name?*, SCM 1985.

P. F. Knitter, *One Earth, Many Religions*, Orbis 1995.

K. Koyama, *Waterbuffalo Theology*, SCM 1974.

H. Kung, *Christianity and the World Religions*, Collins 1987.

H. Kung and J. Moltmann, *Christianity among World Religions*, T. and T. Clark 1986.

C. Lamb, *Belief in a Mixed Society*, Lion 1985.

D. Lockhead, *The Dialogical Imperative*, SCM 1988.

L. Luzbetak, *Catholic Evangelization Today*, ed. by K. Boyack. Paulist Press 1987.

P. Masefield, *Divine Revelation in Pali Buddhism*, Allen & Unwin 1986.

J. Mbiti, *Concepts of God in Africa*, SPCK 1970.

J. Mbiti, *New Testament Eschatology in an African Background*, OUP 1971.

S. Neill, *Christian Faith and Other Faiths*, OUP 1970.

H. A. Netland, *Christianity and the Religions: A Biblical Theology of World Religions*, Wm. Carey Library 1995.

H. A. Netland, *Dissonant Voices; Religious Pluralism and the Question of Truth*, Eerdmans 1991.

J. E. L. Newbigin, *Christian Witness in a Plural Society*, BCC 1977.

J. E. L. Newbigin, *The Open Secret*, SPCK 1978.

B. Nicholls (ed.), *The Unique Christ in our Pluralist World*, Paternoster 1994.

R. Panikkar, *The Unknown Christ of Hinduism*, Darton, Longman & Todd 1968.

G. Parrinder, *Avatar and Incarnation*, Faber & Faber 1970.

W. Petchsongkram, *Talks in the Shade of the Bo Tree*. (No date or publisher cited in the book.)

C. H. Pinnock, *A Wideness in God's Mercy*, Zondervan 1992.

C. H. Pinnock, *The Openness of God*, Paternoster 1994.

A. Race, *Interfaith Encounter*, SCM 2001.

S. Radhakrishnan, *Religion in a Changing World*, Allen & Unwin 1967.

K. Rahner, *Theological Investigations Vols 1–12*, Seabury Press 1972–75.

V. Ramachandra, *Faiths in Conflict? Integrity in a Multicultural World*, IVP 1999.

V. Ramachandra, *The Recovery of Mission: Beyond the Pluralist Paradigm*, Paternoster 1996.

D. Richardson, *Eternity in Their Hearts*, Regal Books 1981.

E. Rommen and H. Netland (eds), *Christianity and the Religions*, Wm. Carey Library 1995.

R. Rousseau (edited by), *Christianity and the Religions of the East*, Ridge Row Press 1982.

S. J. Samartha (edited by), *Faith in the Midst of Faiths*, WCC Geneva 1977.

J. L. Segundo, *The Liberation of Theology*, Gill and Macmillan 1977.

D. Senior and C. Stuhlmueller, *The Biblical Foundations for Mission*, SCM 1983.

C. S. Song, *The Compassionate God*, SCM/Orbis 1982.

C. S. Song, *Third Eye Theology*, Orbis 1979.

J. Stott, *Christian Mission in the Modern World*, Falcon 1975.

J. W. Sweetman, *Islam and Christian Theology*, Lutterworth 1955.

L. Swidler, *The Uniqueness of Jesus: A Dialogue with Paul F. Knitter*, Orbis 1997.

H. Taylor, *The Uniqueness of Christ in a Pluralistic World*, Rutherford House 1994.

J. V. Taylor, *Primal Vision*, ed. by Max Warren, SCM 1963.

P. Van Buren, *A Theology of the Jewish-Christian Reality*, Harper & Row 1987.

J. Verkuyl, *Contemporary Missiology*, Eerdmans 1978.

F. Whaling, *Christian Theology and World Religions*, Marshall Pickering 1986.

C. J. H. Wright, *Thinking Clearly about the Uniqueness of Jesus*, Monarch 1997.